THE DIVINITY OF JESUS

Exploring the Eternal Nature of Jesus

Dr. Maxwell Shimba

Printed by Shimba Publishing LLC
Printed in the United States of America

TABLE OF CONTENTS

INTRODUCTION

The Divinity of Jesus by Dr. Maxwell Shimba

In The Divinity of Jesus, Dr. Maxwell Shimba offers a profound exploration of one of Christianity's most foundational truths: the divine nature of Jesus Christ. Through an in-depth theological study, this book addresses key questions surrounding Jesus' identity as the Son of God and Savior of the world, grounding its insights in the Bible, historical creeds, and Christian thought. Here's what readers can expect from this illuminating work:

1. Biblical Exegesis and Scriptural Foundation

The book delves deeply into Scripture, using verses from both the Old and New Testaments to establish Jesus' divinity. From prophecies in the Hebrew Scriptures to the testimony of the Gospels and Epistles, Dr. Shimba provides a thorough exposition of how the Bible consistently affirms Jesus as fully divine and fully human. Verses like John 1:1-14, Colossians 1:15-20, and Hebrews 1:1-4 serve as key anchors for this exploration.

2. Theological Insights from Early Church Fathers

Dr. Shimba draws on the writings of early church fathers such as Augustine, Athanasius, and Irenaeus, to illustrate how the early Christian community understood and defended the divinity of Jesus. Readers will learn how the early church clarified Jesus' divine nature in the face of heresies and misunderstandings, particularly through the formation of the Nicene Creed.

3. The Role of the Holy Spirit in Revealing Christ's Divinity

A significant portion of the book focuses on the role of the Holy Spirit in testifying to Jesus' divine nature and continuing His work on earth. Readers will gain a deeper understanding of how the Holy Spirit empowers believers to experience the reality of Jesus' authority, resurrection, and eternal reign.

4. Expository Studies with Comprehensive Commentary

With careful attention to detail, Dr. Shimba provides a scholarly yet accessible commentary on key passages of Scripture that affirm Jesus' divine status. His expository approach allows readers to gain clarity on complex theological concepts while offering practical applications for how Jesus' divinity affects Christian life and practice today.

5. Reflections on the Historical Creeds

The Divinity of Jesus reviews how key historical creeds, such as the Nicene and Chalcedonian Creeds, formalized the Christian belief in Jesus' divinity. Readers will learn how these creeds were developed in response to doctrinal challenges and how they remain vital for affirming orthodox Christian beliefs in the modern church.

6. Addressing Contemporary Challenges

Dr. Shimba addresses modern debates and challenges to the doctrine of Jesus' divinity, offering responses rooted in biblical authority and historical Christian teaching. The book engages with contemporary views that question or downplay Jesus' divine nature, reaffirming the traditional Christian stance.

7. Practical Implications for Believers

Finally, readers will come away with a clear understanding of how believing in Jesus' divinity shapes every aspect of the Christian faith. From salvation through Christ to the transformative power of the Holy Spirit, this belief is shown to be central to Christian life and hope. Dr. Shimba highlights the importance of living in the power of Jesus' divinity and the work of the Holy Spirit in daily Christian practice.

The Divinity of Jesus is both a theological treatise and a spiritual guide, designed to deepen the reader's understanding of Christ's divine nature and encourage a richer, more vibrant faith. Whether you are a theologian, a church leader, or a believer seeking to strengthen your faith, this book provides a comprehensive and spiritually enriching journey into the heart of Christian belief.

DR. MAXWELL SHIMBA

CHAPTER 01

THE ETERNAL WORD

1.1 Introduction

The concept of Jesus Christ as the Eternal Word is foundational to Christian theology and central to the understanding of His divinity. The Gospel of John begins with a profound statement that encapsulates this truth: "In the beginning was the Word, and the Word was with God, and the Word was God" (John 1:1). This verse, rich in theological depth, establishes the pre-existence of Jesus Christ, affirming that He is not merely a historical figure or a prophet but the eternal, divine Logos, the very expression of God's nature and will.

1.2 The Pre-existence of Christ

The idea that Jesus existed before His incarnation is a cornerstone of Christian belief. Unlike any other human being, Jesus did not come into existence at the moment of His birth. Instead, He existed eternally with God the Father. The term "Word" (Logos in Greek) used by John is significant because it conveys the concept of divine reason, order, and communication. In both Jewish and Greek thought, Logos represented something much greater than human language; it was the divine principle that governs the cosmos.

John's assertion that "the Word was with God" emphasizes the distinct personhood of Christ, coexisting with God the Father, yet maintaining unity with Him. This coexistence is not a mere proximity but an intimate, relational union within the Godhead. Furthermore, the statement "the Word was God" unequivocally declares the divinity of Jesus. He is not a lesser being or a created entity; He is fully God, sharing the same essence as the Father.

1.3 Biblical Evidence for the Eternal Word

The pre-existence of Jesus is attested to throughout the New Testament. In John 8:58, Jesus Himself declares, "Before Abraham was, I am." This statement not only asserts His existence before Abraham, a patriarch who lived centuries before Christ's earthly life, but it also echoes the divine name revealed to Moses in Exodus 3:14, "I AM WHO I AM." By using the phrase "I am," Jesus aligns Himself with the God of Israel, the eternal, self-existent One.

The Apostle Paul also affirms the pre-existence and divinity of Christ in his letters. In Colossians 1:16-17, Paul writes, "For by Him all things were created that are in heaven and that are on earth, visible and invisible, whether thrones or dominions or principalities or powers. All things were created through Him and for Him. And He is before all things, and in Him all things consist." Here, Paul portrays Jesus not only as pre-existent but as the agent of creation, sustaining the universe by His power.

Hebrews 1:2 further supports this by stating that God "has in these last days spoken to us by His Son, whom He has appointed heir of all things, through whom also He made the worlds." Jesus is the one through whom God created everything, reinforcing His eternal nature and divine authority.

1.4 The Logos in Old Testament Revelation

Although the full revelation of the Logos is found in the New Testament, the concept is rooted in the Old Testament. Various passages hint at the presence of a divine person who acts on behalf of God and embodies His word. For example, in Proverbs 8:22-31, Wisdom is personified and described as being present with God before the creation of the world, participating in the creation process. While not a direct reference to Christ, early Christians saw this as a foreshadowing of the Logos.

Furthermore, the "Angel of the Lord" in the Old Testament often speaks as God, identifies with God, and yet is distinct from God (e.g., Genesis 16:7-13; Exodus 3:2-6). Early Christian theologians interpreted these appearances as pre-incarnate manifestations of Christ, the Logos.

1.5 The Incarnation: The Word Made Flesh

John 1:14 states, "And the Word became flesh and dwelt among us, and we beheld His glory, the glory as of the only begotten of the Father, full of grace and truth." The incarnation is the pivotal moment where the eternal Word entered human history. The divine Logos, who existed with God from the beginning, took on human nature and lived among us. This profound mystery—God becoming man—is central to the Christian faith.

The incarnation reveals the depths of God's love and the extent of His desire to redeem humanity. The eternal Word did not remain distant or detached from His creation; instead, He entered into the human experience, sharing in our sufferings, joys, and limitations, yet without sin. In doing so, He provided the perfect revelation of God and the means for our salvation.

1.6 Theological Implications of the Eternal Word

Understanding Jesus as the Eternal Word has significant theological implications. It affirms that Jesus is not merely a messenger or a moral teacher but God Himself, worthy of worship and obedience. His pre-existence and role in creation establish His authority over all things, including life and death.

Moreover, the eternal nature of Christ provides the basis for our hope in eternal life. As the one who is eternal, Jesus offers eternal life to those who believe in Him. He is the source of all life, both physical and spiritual, and through Him, we are united with the eternal God.

The doctrine of the Eternal Word also emphasizes the continuity of God's plan throughout history. The same Word who was with God in the beginning is the one who became flesh to redeem us. This underscores the consistency and faithfulness of God, who has worked through the ages to bring about His purposes.

1.7 Conclusion

The concept of Jesus as the Eternal Word is central to the Christian understanding of His divinity. From the opening verses of John's Gospel to the teachings of the apostles, the Bible consistently presents Jesus as the pre-existent, divine Logos, who was with God and was God. His incarnation as the Word made flesh is the ultimate expression of God's love and the definitive revelation of His nature.

As we reflect on the Eternal Word, we are drawn into a deeper appreciation of who Jesus is and what He has done for us. He is the Alpha and Omega, the beginning and the end, the one through whom all things were made and the one who sustains all things. In Him, we find the fullness of life and the assurance of eternal hope.

Jesus as the Son of God

2.1 Introduction

The title "Son of God" is one of the most profound and significant designations given to Jesus Christ in the New Testament. This title encapsulates both His unique relationship with God the Father and His divine nature. Understanding what it means for Jesus to be the Son of God is crucial for grasping the core of Christian doctrine and the identity of Jesus as the Messiah, the Savior of the world. In this chapter, we will explore the meaning and significance of this title, its biblical foundations, and its implications for faith and theology.

2.2 The Biblical Foundation of the Title

The title "Son of God" is rooted in both Old and New Testament scriptures. In the Old Testament, the term is occasionally used to describe Israel (Exodus 4:22-23), the Davidic king (2 Samuel 7:14), and even angels (Job 1:6). However, these usages were more metaphorical and did not imply a divine nature. The New Testament, however, reveals a much deeper and more profound understanding of this title when applied to Jesus.

In the New Testament, Jesus is explicitly referred to as the "Son of God" in multiple instances, highlighting His unique and unparalleled relationship with God the Father. One of the most notable affirmations comes at Jesus' baptism, where a voice from heaven declares, "This is my beloved Son, in whom I am well pleased" (Matthew 3:17). This divine proclamation not only identifies Jesus as the Son of God but also affirms His mission and divine approval.

Another significant moment occurs at the Transfiguration, where God's voice again affirms Jesus' sonship: "This is my beloved Son, in whom I am well pleased; hear Him!" (Matthew 17:5). These divine endorsements set Jesus apart from all others, marking Him as the unique, eternal Son of God.

2.3 The Sonship of Jesus: More Than a Title

The title "Son of God" does not merely indicate a filial relationship but also signifies Jesus' divine nature and authority. In the cultural and religious context of the time, calling someone the "Son of God" would be tantamount to equating them with God Himself. This is evident in the reaction of the Jewish leaders when Jesus claimed God as His Father: "Therefore the Jews sought all the more to kill Him, because He not only broke the Sabbath but also said that God was His Father, making Himself equal with God" (John 5:18).

Jesus' sonship is unique in several ways:

1. Eternal Sonship: Unlike any other figure referred to as a "son of God," Jesus' sonship is eternal. He was not adopted or created as a son but is eternally begotten of the Father. This is affirmed in John 1:18, where Jesus is described as "the only begotten Son, who is in the bosom of the Father." This eternal generation indicates that Jesus shares the same divine essence as the Father, making Him co-equal and co-eternal with God.

2. Divine Authority: As the Son of God, Jesus possesses divine authority over all creation. This authority is evident in His teachings, miracles, and, ultimately, His resurrection. In John 10:30, Jesus states, "I and My Father are one," emphasizing His unity with the Father in purpose and essence. This divine authority also means that Jesus has the

power to forgive sins, as demonstrated in Mark 2:5-7, where He heals a paralytic and forgives his sins, leading the scribes to accuse Him of blasphemy because only God can forgive sins.

3. Revelation of the Father: Jesus, as the Son of God, perfectly reveals the Father to humanity. In John 14:9, Jesus tells Philip, "He who has seen Me has seen the Father." This statement underscores the idea that Jesus is the exact representation of God's nature, as described in Hebrews 1:3: "He is the radiance of His glory and the exact representation of His nature." Through Jesus, humanity encounters the fullness of God's character, love, and will.

2.4 The Son of God in the Synoptic Gospels

The Synoptic Gospels (Matthew, Mark, and Luke) provide numerous instances where Jesus is identified as the Son of God. In addition to the divine affirmations at His baptism and Transfiguration, demons frequently acknowledge Jesus as the Son of God, recognizing His authority over them (Matthew 8:29; Mark 3:11). This recognition by spiritual beings further attests to Jesus' divine status.

Moreover, the title "Son of God" is closely linked to Jesus' messianic role. In Matthew 16:16, Peter's confession, "You are the Christ, the Son of the living God," highlights the connection between Jesus' messianic mission and His divine sonship. Jesus affirms Peter's confession, stating that it was revealed to him by God the Father (Matthew 16:17), emphasizing the divine origin and truth of this title.

2.5 The Son of God in the Gospel of John

The Gospel of John places particular emphasis on Jesus as the Son of God. The prologue of John (John 1:1-18) introduces Jesus as the Word who was with God and was God, setting the stage for the unfolding revelation of His divine sonship. Throughout the Gospel, Jesus refers to God as His Father, highlighting their unique relationship.

John 3:16, one of the most well-known verses in the Bible, encapsulates the significance of Jesus as the Son of God: "For God so loved the world that He gave His only begotten Son, that whoever believes in Him should not perish but have everlasting life." This verse underscores the sacrificial love of God in sending His Son and the salvific purpose of Jesus' mission.

In John 5:19-23, Jesus elaborates on His relationship with the Father, stating that He can do nothing by Himself but only what He sees the Father doing. He also asserts that the Father has entrusted all judgment to the Son so that all may honor the Son just as they honor the Father. This passage reveals the depth of the unity between the Father and the Son and the divine authority vested in Jesus.

2.6 Theological Implications of Jesus as the Son of God

Understanding Jesus as the Son of God carries profound theological implications:

1. Christology: The title "Son of God" is central to Christology, the study of the person and work of Christ. It affirms Jesus' divinity, His pre-existence, and His unique relationship with the Father. This understanding is vital for a correct interpretation of who Jesus is and what He accomplished through His life, death, and resurrection.

2. Salvation: Jesus' identity as the Son of God is directly connected to His ability to save. As the divine Son, He possesses the power to atone for sin, reconcile humanity to God, and grant eternal life. Only a Savior who is fully God can bridge the gap between a holy God and sinful humanity.

3. Trinitarian Doctrine: The title "Son of God" is integral to the doctrine of the Trinity. It highlights the distinction of persons within the Godhead while maintaining the unity of essence. Jesus' sonship demonstrates the relational aspect of the Trinity, where the Father, Son, and Holy Spirit exist in perfect harmony and love.

4. Worship and Devotion: Recognizing Jesus as the Son of God compels believers to worship Him as Lord and God. The acknowledgment of His divine sonship leads to a life of devotion, obedience, and reverence, as believers respond to the revelation of who He is.

2.7 Conclusion

The title "Son of God" is not merely a descriptor but a profound affirmation of Jesus' divine nature and unique relationship with God the Father. It encapsulates the essence of who Jesus is—eternally begotten, possessing divine authority, and perfectly revealing the Father to humanity. This understanding is essential for a full appreciation of Jesus' identity and His role in the salvation of the world.

As we reflect on Jesus as the Son of God, we are invited to deepen our faith and devotion, recognizing that in Him, we encounter the fullness of God's love, grace, and truth. This title, rich in meaning and significance, stands at the heart of Christian belief, shaping our understanding of Jesus and our relationship with Him.

The Purpose of the Book

3.1 Introduction

The divinity of Jesus Christ is the cornerstone of Christian faith. It is not merely a theological concept but the very foundation upon which the entirety of Christianity is built. This book aims to explore and affirm the divinity of Jesus Christ, as well as to demonstrate why recognizing and understanding this truth is crucial for believers. By delving into the biblical, historical, and theological aspects of Jesus' divine nature, this book seeks to strengthen the reader's faith and deepen their relationship with Christ.

3.2 The Centrality of Jesus' Divinity in Christian Faith

At the heart of Christianity lies the belief that Jesus Christ is not just a prophet, teacher, or moral example but the incarnate Son of God—fully divine and fully human. This belief distinguishes Christianity from all other religions and philosophies. It is what makes Christianity unique and what gives it its transformative power.

The significance of Jesus' divinity is evident throughout the New Testament. The Gospels, the writings of Paul, and the teachings of the early Church all emphasize that Jesus is God in the flesh, come to redeem humanity. This understanding is crucial because it directly affects how Christians view salvation, worship, and their relationship with God.

If Jesus were merely a human being, even an extraordinarily good one, His death on the cross would not have the power to atone for the sins of the world. It is precisely because Jesus is divine that His sacrifice is sufficient to cover the sins of all people, providing a way for humanity to be reconciled to God. The recognition of Jesus' divinity is, therefore, essential for understanding the nature of salvation.

Moreover, the divinity of Jesus informs the Christian practice of worship. Christians do not merely follow the teachings of a wise man; they worship Jesus as Lord and God. The early Church was willing to suffer persecution and martyrdom for the confession that "Jesus is Lord," a confession that would be meaningless if Jesus were not divine. The act of worship is directed toward God alone, and the fact that Jesus is worshiped by Christians throughout history affirms His divine status.

3.3 The Role of the Holy Spirit in Revealing Jesus' Divinity

The Holy Spirit plays a crucial role in revealing the divinity of Jesus to believers. As Jesus Himself stated, the Spirit will "guide you into all truth" and "will take of what is Mine and declare it to you" (John 16:13-14). The Spirit's work is to glorify Christ and to lead believers into a deeper understanding of His nature and mission.

Recognizing Jesus' divinity is not merely an intellectual exercise; it is a spiritual revelation that comes through the work of the Holy Spirit. This book seeks to align with the

Spirit's work by providing a biblical and theological framework that supports and deepens the reader's understanding of Jesus' divine nature.

The purpose of this book, therefore, is not just to present doctrinal truths but to facilitate a spiritual encounter with the living Christ. Through the study of Scripture and the guidance of the Holy Spirit, readers are invited to see Jesus as He truly is—the eternal Son of God, worthy of all honor, glory, and praise.

3.4 Strengthening Faith Through Understanding

One of the primary purposes of this book is to strengthen the faith of believers by providing a clear and comprehensive understanding of Jesus' divinity. In a world where faith is often challenged by skepticism, secularism, and alternative spiritualities, it is essential for Christians to be firmly rooted in the truth of who Jesus is.

A robust understanding of Jesus' divinity equips believers to withstand the pressures and doubts that may arise in their spiritual journey. It also enables them to confidently share their faith with others, providing answers to questions and objections that may be raised by those who do not yet know Christ.

Furthermore, understanding Jesus' divinity deepens the believer's appreciation for the love and grace of God. The realization that the Creator of the universe took on human flesh, lived among us, and died for our sins is a profound truth that should inspire awe and gratitude. It reminds us of the lengths to which God has gone to redeem us and how much He values each of us.

3.5 Addressing Contemporary Challenges to Jesus' Divinity

In contemporary society, there are many challenges to the belief in Jesus' divinity. Some view Jesus as merely a historical figure, a moral teacher, or a revolutionary leader. Others question the reliability of the biblical accounts or reinterpret them in ways that diminish or deny His divine nature.

This book seeks to address these challenges by presenting a clear and compelling case for Jesus' divinity based on biblical evidence, historical context, and theological reflection. By engaging with these issues, the book aims to equip believers with the knowledge and confidence they need to stand firm in their faith and to articulate their beliefs in a way that is both intellectually credible and spiritually enriching.

In addition to addressing external challenges, the book also seeks to help believers overcome internal doubts and struggles. Many Christians may experience moments of uncertainty or confusion about their faith, particularly in a culture that is increasingly skeptical of religious claims. By providing a deeper understanding of who Jesus is, this book aims to help believers navigate these challenges and emerge with a stronger, more resilient faith.

3.6 The Transformative Power of Recognizing Jesus' Divinity

Finally, this book is written with the conviction that recognizing Jesus' divinity has the power to transform lives. When we understand that Jesus is not just a figure from history but the living God who is actively involved in our lives, it changes everything.

Recognizing Jesus' divinity leads to a deeper commitment to following Him. It challenges us to live lives that reflect His lordship, to pursue holiness, and to love others as He has loved us. It also brings comfort and assurance, knowing that the one we follow is not just a human leader but the eternal Son of God, who has conquered sin and death and who reigns as Lord of all.

Moreover, recognizing Jesus' divinity opens up the possibility of a personal relationship with God. Through Jesus, we are invited into the very life of the Trinity, to know God as Father, Son, and Holy Spirit. This relationship is the source of all true joy, peace, and fulfillment, and it is available to all who acknowledge Jesus as Lord and Savior.

3.7 Conclusion

The purpose of this book is to affirm, explore, and deepen the reader's understanding of the divinity of Jesus Christ. This truth is central to the Christian faith, shaping our understanding of salvation, worship, and our relationship with God. By providing a biblical, historical, and theological foundation for this belief, the book aims to strengthen the faith of believers, address contemporary challenges, and facilitate a deeper spiritual encounter with Christ.

As you read and reflect on the contents of this book, may the Holy Spirit guide you into all truth, and may you come to a fuller recognition of Jesus Christ as the eternal Son of God, the Savior of the world, and the Lord of all creation.

CHAPTER 02

THE CONTEXT OF JOHN CHAPTER 16

The Setting: The Last Supper and Jesus' Final Discourse

4.1 Introduction

The Last Supper and Jesus' final discourse are pivotal moments in the Gospel narrative, setting the stage for the culmination of Jesus' earthly ministry. These events, recorded in detail in the Gospel of John (chapters 13-17), provide a profound insight into Jesus' heart and mind as He prepares to face His imminent crucifixion. The setting of the Last Supper and the final discourse is not just a backdrop for Jesus' teachings but a deeply significant moment that reveals His divinity, His love for His disciples, and His ultimate purpose in the salvation of humanity.

4.2 The Last Supper: A Time of Intimacy and Revelation

The Last Supper, also known as the Lord's Supper, is one of the most intimate moments Jesus shares with His disciples. It is a time when He gathers His closest followers to celebrate the Passover, a feast that commemorates Israel's deliverance from Egypt. However, this meal takes on new meaning as Jesus uses it to institute the New Covenant and to reveal the deep truths about His mission and identity.

4.2.1 The Significance of the Passover

The Passover was a central observance in Jewish life, commemorating God's deliverance of the Israelites from slavery in Egypt. The ritual involved the sacrifice of a lamb and the eating of unleavened bread, symbolizing the haste with which the Israelites left Egypt. By choosing to celebrate the Passover with His disciples, Jesus connects His impending death with the themes of deliverance and sacrifice.

However, Jesus transforms the traditional Passover meal into something entirely new. He takes the bread and the wine, elements of the Passover meal, and reinterprets them as symbols of His body and blood, which will be given for the salvation of the world. This act institutes the Eucharist, or

Communion, a sacrament that Christians continue to observe in remembrance of Christ's sacrifice.

4.2.2 The Washing of the Disciples' Feet

One of the most striking and unexpected moments of the Last Supper is Jesus' act of washing His disciples' feet. In John 13:1-17, Jesus, knowing that His hour had come, rises from the table, lays aside His garments, and begins to wash the feet of His disciples. This act of humility is a powerful demonstration of servant leadership, a model that Jesus sets for all who would follow Him.

The washing of feet was a task typically performed by the lowest servant in the household. For Jesus, the Master and Teacher, to perform this act was shocking to the disciples, particularly to Peter, who initially refuses to let Jesus wash his feet. However, Jesus insists, saying, "If I do not wash you, you have no part with Me" (John 13:8). This statement highlights the necessity of spiritual cleansing and the importance of humility in the Kingdom of God.

Through this act, Jesus not only demonstrates His love for His disciples but also foreshadows the greater act of service that He will perform on the cross. The washing of the disciples' feet symbolizes the cleansing from sin that Jesus' sacrificial death will accomplish, and it calls His followers to live lives of humility and service.

4.2.3 The Betrayal Foretold

The Last Supper is also marked by the foretelling of Judas' betrayal. In John 13:21-30, Jesus reveals that one of His own disciples will betray Him. This announcement creates a sense of tension and sorrow among the disciples, who are shocked to hear that one of them would betray their Master.

Jesus' awareness of the betrayal, and His calm acceptance of it, underscores His divinity and His submission to the Father's will. He knows that His betrayal and subsequent suffering are part of the divine plan for the redemption of humanity. By identifying Judas as the betrayer, Jesus also fulfills the prophecy found in Psalm 41:9: "Even my close friend, someone I trusted, one who shared my bread, has turned against me."

The knowledge of His impending betrayal and suffering does not deter Jesus from His mission. Instead, it strengthens His resolve to complete the work that the Father has given Him to do. This moment serves as a powerful reminder of Jesus' obedience and love, even in the face of treachery and pain.

4.3 Jesus' Final Discourse: A Farewell Address

After the events of the Last Supper, Jesus delivers His final discourse to the disciples, recorded in John 14-16. This discourse, often referred to as the "Farewell Discourse," is a deeply personal and theological reflection on the relationship between Jesus, the Father, and the disciples. It is in this discourse that Jesus provides His followers with comfort, instruction, and the promise of the Holy Spirit.

4.3.1 Comfort for Troubled Hearts

As Jesus begins His final discourse, He immediately addresses the anxiety and fear that the disciples are experiencing. He knows that His imminent departure will leave them feeling abandoned and confused. In John 14:1, He says, "Let not your heart be troubled; you believe in God, believe also in Me." Jesus reassures them that His departure is not the end but the beginning of something greater.

Jesus speaks of preparing a place for them in His Father's house and promises that He will return to take them to be with Him (John 14:2-3). This promise of eternal life with God provides the disciples with hope and comfort in the midst of uncertainty. It also reinforces the idea that Jesus' mission extends beyond His earthly life, pointing to the eternal significance of His work.

4.3.2 The Promise of the Holy Spirit

One of the most important aspects of Jesus' final discourse is the promise of the Holy Spirit. Jesus assures the disciples that He will not leave them as orphans but will send the Holy Spirit, the "Helper" or "Comforter," to be with them forever (John 14:16-17). The Holy Spirit will teach them all things, remind them of Jesus' words, and guide them into all truth (John 14:26; 16:13).

The promise of the Holy Spirit is a central theme in the Farewell Discourse, as it highlights the continuity of Jesus' presence and ministry after His departure. The Spirit will empower the disciples to carry on Jesus' work and to bear witness to His life, death, and resurrection. This promise is not only for the original disciples but for all believers, ensuring that the Church will be guided by the Spirit throughout the ages.

4.3.3 The Call to Abide in Christ

In John 15, Jesus uses the metaphor of the vine and the branches to illustrate the relationship between Himself and His disciples. He exhorts them to "abide in Me, and I in you" (John 15:4), emphasizing the importance of remaining in close, intimate fellowship with Him. Just as a branch cannot bear fruit unless it remains connected to the vine, so the disciples cannot bear spiritual fruit unless they remain connected to Christ.

This call to abide in Christ is a call to live in constant dependence on Him, drawing strength, guidance, and life from His presence. It is a call to obedience and love, as Jesus commands His disciples to love one another as He has loved them (John 15:12). The metaphor of the vine and the branches also reinforces the idea that Jesus is the source of all spiritual life and vitality, and that apart from Him, the disciples can do nothing (John 15:5).

4.3.4 The Reality of Persecution

In His final discourse, Jesus does not shy away from the reality of persecution. He warns the disciples that they will face opposition and hatred from the world because of their association with Him (John 15:18-20). However, He also provides them with the assurance that they are not alone in their suffering. The Holy Spirit will testify on their behalf, and they will have the strength to endure (John 15:26-27).

Jesus' words about persecution are a sobering reminder that following Him often involves sacrifice and suffering. Yet, He also reminds the disciples that their suffering is not in vain. It is part of the cost of discipleship, and it serves to refine their faith and witness to the world.

4.3.5 The Promise of Joy and Peace

Despite the challenges and trials that lie ahead, Jesus promises His disciples a deep and abiding joy and peace. In John 16:20-22, He compares their coming sorrow to the pain of childbirth, which is followed by the joy of a new life. He assures them that their grief will be turned to joy, a joy that no one can take away.

Jesus also promises them peace, not as the world gives, but His own divine peace (John 14:27). This peace is not the absence of trouble but the presence of God in the midst of it. It is the peace that comes from knowing that Jesus has overcome the world and that His victory is secure (John 16:33).

4.4 The High Priestly Prayer: Jesus' Prayer for His Disciples

The final chapter of Jesus' discourse is His High Priestly Prayer, recorded in John 17. In this prayer, Jesus prays for Himself, His disciples, and all future believers. This prayer reveals Jesus' deep love for His followers and His desire for their unity, protection, and sanctification.

4.4.1 Jesus Prays for Himself

In the opening verses of the prayer, Jesus prays for Himself, asking the Father to glorify Him so that He may glorify the Father (John 17:1). This request is not a selfish one but a recognition that the hour of His crucifixion has come and that through His suffering and death, God's glory will

be revealed. Jesus' prayer also reflects His awareness of the completion of His earthly mission and His anticipation of returning to the Father's presence (John 17:4-5).

4.4.2 Jesus Prays for His Disciples

Jesus then turns His attention to His disciples, praying for their protection and unity (John 17:9-11). He asks the Father to keep them in His name, to protect them from the evil one, and to sanctify them in the truth (John 17:15-17). Jesus knows that His departure will leave the disciples vulnerable, but He entrusts them to the Father's care, confident that they will be preserved and empowered to continue His work.

4.4.3 Jesus Prays for Future Believers

In the final section of the prayer, Jesus prays for all who will believe in Him through the testimony of the disciples (John 17:20-21). He prays for their unity, asking that they may be one, just as He and the Father are one. This unity is not merely organizational but a profound spiritual oneness that reflects the unity of the Trinity. Jesus' prayer for future believers highlights His concern for the Church throughout the ages and His desire for its witness to the world.

4.5 Conclusion

The Last Supper and Jesus' final discourse are among the most significant events in the Gospel of John. They provide a window into Jesus' heart and mind as He prepares to face the cross. These moments are filled with deep theological truths, expressions of love, and promises of hope that continue to resonate with believers today.

As we reflect on the setting of the Last Supper and the final discourse, we are reminded of the importance of abiding in Christ, the necessity of spiritual humility and service, and the assurance of the Holy Spirit's presence in our lives. Jesus' words and actions during these final moments with His disciples reveal His divinity, His love, and His commitment to the mission of redemption. They call us to a deeper understanding of who Jesus is and what it means to follow Him, even in the face of difficulty and uncertainty.

The Last Supper and the final discourse are not just historical events but living realities that continue to shape the life of the Church and the faith of believers. As we meditate on these passages, may we be drawn into a closer relationship with Christ, the eternal Son of God, who loved us and gave Himself for us.

Understanding the Audience: Who Were the Disciples, and Why Was This Message Crucial for Them?

5.1 Introduction

The audience to whom Jesus addressed His final discourse was not an ordinary group of people but His closest followers—the disciples. These men had walked with Jesus for three years, witnessing His miracles, hearing His teachings, and sharing in His ministry. Understanding who these disciples were and why Jesus' message was crucial for them is key to grasping the full impact of the Last Supper and the final discourse. In this chapter, we will explore the identity of the disciples, their role in Jesus' ministry, and the importance of the message that Jesus conveyed to them during these final hours.

5.2 The Identity of the Disciples

The term "disciple" refers to a learner or follower, and in the context of the Gospels, it specifically refers to those who followed Jesus and learned from His teachings. Among the larger group of followers, Jesus selected twelve men whom He designated as His apostles. These twelve were given special authority and responsibility to carry on Jesus' mission after His departure. The twelve disciples—Peter, James, John, Andrew, Philip, Bartholomew (Nathanael), Matthew, Thomas, James the son of Alphaeus, Thaddaeus (Judas the son of James), Simon the Zealot, and Judas Iscariot—were ordinary men chosen for an extraordinary purpose.

5.2.1 Peter, James, and John: The Inner Circle

Within the group of twelve, three disciples—Peter, James, and John—were particularly close to Jesus. These three were present at significant moments in Jesus' ministry that others were not, such as the Transfiguration (Matthew 17:1-9), the raising of Jairus's daughter (Mark 5:37-43), and Jesus' agonizing prayer in the Garden of Gethsemane (Matthew 26:36-46). Peter, known for his boldness and impulsive nature, would later emerge as a leader among the apostles. James and John, the sons of Zebedee, were also known as the "Sons of Thunder" due to their passionate personalities (Mark 3:17).

These three disciples had a unique closeness to Jesus, and their experiences with Him deepened their understanding of His mission and identity. However, like all the disciples, they struggled at times to fully grasp the implications of Jesus' teachings and the nature of His Kingdom.

5.2.2 The Broader Group of Disciples

The other nine disciples also played crucial roles in Jesus' ministry. Each had their own background and personality, contributing to the diverse nature of the group. Matthew, for instance, was a tax collector, a profession despised by many Jews, yet he was called to follow Jesus (Matthew 9:9). Simon the Zealot, on the other hand, was likely a member of a radical Jewish sect that sought to overthrow Roman rule. Despite their different backgrounds, these men were united by their commitment to follow Jesus and to learn from Him.

Judas Iscariot, the disciple who would eventually betray Jesus, was also part of this group. His presence among the disciples highlights the complexity and tension within the group. Judas's betrayal would become a central element in the events leading up to Jesus' crucifixion, demonstrating the tragic consequences of rejecting the truth that Jesus revealed.

5.3 The Role of the Disciples in Jesus' Ministry

The disciples were not just passive followers; they were active participants in Jesus' ministry. Jesus commissioned them to preach the Gospel, heal the sick, and cast out demons (Matthew 10:1-8). They were entrusted with the message of the Kingdom of God and were sent out as representatives of Jesus to the towns and villages of Israel. Through their experiences, the disciples learned about faith, dependence on God, and the cost of discipleship.

However, the disciples were also often portrayed in the Gospels as struggling to understand Jesus' teachings fully. They frequently misunderstood His parables, questioned His decisions, and even doubted His identity as the Messiah. For example, after Jesus calmed the storm, the disciples marveled and asked, "Who can this be, that even the wind and the sea obey Him?" (Mark 4:41). Their journey of faith was marked by moments of revelation and confusion, boldness and fear, understanding and doubt.

5.3.1 The Disciples' Growing Awareness of Jesus' Identity

Throughout their time with Jesus, the disciples' understanding of His identity gradually deepened. Early in their journey, they recognized Jesus as a great teacher and miracle worker, but it took time for them to fully grasp that He was the Son of God. Peter's confession at Caesarea Philippi, where he declared, "You are the Christ, the Son of the living God" (Matthew 16:16), was a pivotal moment in this journey. However, even after this confession, the disciples struggled to understand the implications of Jesus' mission, particularly His predictions of His suffering and death.

Jesus' final discourse was delivered against the backdrop of this growing but incomplete understanding. The disciples needed to be prepared for the events that were about to unfold—Jesus' arrest, crucifixion, and resurrection—and for their future role as the leaders of the early Church. Jesus' words at the Last Supper were intended to fortify their faith, clarify their mission, and assure them of His continuing presence through the Holy Spirit.

5.4 Why This Message Was Crucial for the Disciples

The message Jesus delivered during the Last Supper and in His final discourse was of utmost importance to the disciples for several reasons:

5.4.1 Preparing for Jesus' Departure

Jesus knew that His time with the disciples was drawing to a close. He had repeatedly told them that He would be betrayed, suffer, and die, but the reality of His departure was difficult for them to accept. The final discourse was Jesus' way of preparing the disciples for what was to come. He needed to reassure them that His death was not the end, but the fulfillment of His mission and the beginning of something new—the era of the Holy Spirit.

Jesus spoke to them about His impending departure in a way that was both realistic and comforting. He did not downplay the pain and sorrow they would experience, but He also offered them hope, promising that He would send the Holy Spirit to guide, comfort, and empower them (John 14:16-17). This message was crucial because it helped the disciples to see beyond the immediate crisis of the crucifixion to the larger plan of God's redemption.

5.4.2 The Promise of the Holy Spirit

One of the central themes of Jesus' final discourse was the promise of the Holy Spirit. The disciples had experienced Jesus' physical presence with them, but Jesus wanted them to understand that His presence would continue with them in a new and powerful way through the Holy Spirit. The Spirit would teach them all things, remind them of Jesus' teachings, and empower them to fulfill the mission that He had entrusted to them (John 14:26; 16:13).

This promise was crucial for the disciples because it ensured that they would not be left to carry out their mission on their own. The Holy Spirit would equip them to face the challenges ahead, to bear witness to the truth of the Gospel, and to build the Church. The promise of the Holy Spirit also affirmed the continuity of Jesus' ministry—what He began in His earthly life would be carried on through the work of the Spirit in and through the disciples.

5.4.3 The Call to Unity and Love

Another key aspect of Jesus' message was the call to unity and love among the disciples. Jesus knew that the trials and persecutions they would face could potentially divide them. He emphasized the importance of loving one another as He had loved them, stating that this love would be the hallmark of their discipleship (John 13:34-35). He also prayed for their unity, asking the Father to make them one, just as He and the Father are one (John 17:20-23).

This call to unity and love was crucial because it would be the foundation of the disciples' witness to the world. Their love for one another would reflect the love of Christ and would serve as a powerful testimony to the reality of the Gospel. In a world that would often be hostile to their message, the unity of the disciples would be a source of strength and a sign of the truth they proclaimed.

5.4.4 The Reality of Persecution and Suffering

Jesus did not shy away from the reality that the disciples would face persecution and suffering because of their association with Him. He warned them that they would be hated by the world, just as He was hated (John 15:18-20). However, He also reassured them that they would not face these trials alone. The Holy Spirit would be with them, and He had already overcome the world (John 16:33).

This message was crucial because it prepared the disciples for the challenges that lay ahead. By acknowledging the reality of suffering and persecution, Jesus strengthened their resolve and encouraged them to remain faithful, knowing that their suffering was part of the path of discipleship and that they would share in His victory.

5.5 The Disciples' Response to Jesus' Final Discourse

The disciples' response to Jesus' final discourse was a mixture of confusion, sorrow, and eventually, understanding and faith. Initially, they struggled to comprehend the full meaning of Jesus' words, particularly His references to His departure and the coming of the Holy Spirit. They were saddened by the prospect of losing their Master, and their questions reflected their uncertainty (John 14:5, 8, 22).

However, after Jesus' resurrection and the outpouring of the Holy Spirit at Pentecost, the disciples' understanding was transformed. The Holy Spirit brought to their remembrance all that Jesus had taught them and empowered them to proclaim the Gospel with boldness and clarity (Acts 2). The message that Jesus delivered during the Last Supper and in His final discourse became the foundation of their ministry and the source of their strength as they spread the message of Jesus' death and resurrection to the ends of the earth.

5.6 Conclusion

The disciples were the chosen audience for Jesus' final discourse, and the message He delivered to them was crucial for their faith, mission, and future. These ordinary men were called to an extraordinary task, and Jesus used His final moments with them to prepare them for the challenges and opportunities that lay ahead. By understanding who the disciples were and why this message was so important for them, we gain a deeper appreciation of the significance of the Last Supper and the final discourse.

As we reflect on the disciples' journey and their response to Jesus' words, we are reminded that we, too, are called to be followers of Christ, empowered by the Holy Spirit, united in love, and committed to the mission of spreading the Gospel. The message that Jesus delivered to His disciples is as relevant for us today as it was for them, calling us to a deeper understanding of His identity, a greater dependence on the Holy Spirit, and a steadfast commitment to His mission in the world.

The Promise of the Holy Spirit: Jesus Preparing the Disciples for His Departure

6.1 Introduction

As Jesus approached the end of His earthly ministry, He was fully aware of the challenges and uncertainties that His imminent departure would bring to His disciples. These men, who had walked closely with Him for three years, would soon face a world without His physical presence. Understanding their fears and concerns, Jesus made a crucial promise: the coming of the Holy Spirit. This promise was not just a consolation but a profound assurance that His presence and power would continue to be with them, enabling them to carry on His mission. In this chapter, we will explore the significance of Jesus' promise of the Holy Spirit, how He prepared the disciples for His departure, and the transformative impact of the Holy Spirit on their lives and ministry.

6.2 The Necessity of Jesus' Departure

Before delving into the promise of the Holy Spirit, it is essential to understand why Jesus' departure was necessary. Throughout His ministry, Jesus had repeatedly hinted at His coming death, resurrection, and ascension. The disciples, however, struggled to comprehend why their Master, whom they believed to be the Messiah, would leave them.

6.2.1 Jesus' Death and Resurrection: Fulfillment of Prophecy

Jesus' death was not a tragic end but a fulfillment of God's redemptive plan. As prophesied in the Old Testament, the Messiah had to suffer, die, and rise again to atone for the sins of humanity (Isaiah 53; Psalm 22). Jesus' departure through death and resurrection was the ultimate act of love and obedience, opening the way for humanity to be reconciled to God.

However, this departure was not the end of Jesus' relationship with His disciples. In fact, it marked the beginning of a new phase in which they would experience His presence in a more profound and intimate way through the Holy Spirit.

6.2.2 The Ascension: Preparing the Way for the Holy Spirit

Jesus' ascension into heaven was a necessary step for the coming of the Holy Spirit. In John 16:7, Jesus tells His disciples, "Nevertheless I tell you the truth: it is to your advantage that I go away; for if I do not go away, the Helper will not come to you; but if I depart, I will send Him to you." This statement underscores the importance of Jesus' departure in the divine plan. The ascension allowed Jesus to assume His rightful place at the right hand of the Father and to send the Holy Spirit to empower and guide His followers.

6.3 The Promise of the Holy Spirit

The promise of the Holy Spirit is one of the central themes in Jesus' final discourse. He repeatedly reassured His disciples that although He was leaving them physically, He would not leave them alone. The Holy Spirit, also referred to as the Helper, Comforter, or Advocate, would come to them, continuing the work that Jesus had begun.

6.3.1 The Role of the Holy Spirit

Jesus described the Holy Spirit as the one who would fulfill several vital roles in the lives of the disciples:

- Teacher and Reminder: Jesus promised that the Holy Spirit would teach the disciples all things and bring to their remembrance all that He had taught them (John 14:26). This role was crucial because, as the disciples faced the challenges of ministry and the pressures of the world, they needed to be reminded of Jesus' teachings and guided into a deeper understanding of the truth.

- Guide into All Truth: The Holy Spirit would guide the disciples into all truth, revealing the full meaning of Jesus' teachings and the implications of His death and resurrection (John 16:13). This guidance was essential for the disciples to accurately proclaim the Gospel and to navigate the complexities of their mission.

- Convicting the World: Jesus also said that the Holy Spirit would convict the world of sin, righteousness, and judgment (John 16:8-11). This role highlights the Spirit's work in the world, bringing people to an awareness of their need for salvation and revealing the righteousness of Christ and the reality of judgment.

- Glorifying Christ: The Holy Spirit's primary purpose is to glorify Christ by taking what belongs to Him and declaring it to the disciples (John 16:14). This means that the Spirit's work is always Christ-centered, pointing believers to Jesus and making His presence and power real in their lives.

6.3.2 The Indwelling Presence of the Holy Spirit

One of the most significant aspects of the Holy Spirit's coming was His indwelling presence in the lives of believers. Jesus promised that the Holy Spirit would not only be with the disciples but would be in them (John 14:17). This indwelling presence marked a profound shift in the way God related to His people. In the Old Testament, the Holy Spirit would come upon certain individuals temporarily for specific purposes. However, under the New Covenant, the Holy Spirit would permanently dwell within every believer, empowering them to live according to God's will and to fulfill the mission of spreading the Gospel.

The indwelling of the Holy Spirit also meant that the disciples would never be alone. Even though Jesus would no longer be with them physically, His presence through the Holy Spirit would be even more intimate and powerful. The Spirit would be their constant companion, guiding, comforting, and empowering them in every aspect of their lives.

6.3.3 The Outpouring of the Holy Spirit at Pentecost

The fulfillment of Jesus' promise of the Holy Spirit occurred on the day of Pentecost, as recorded in Acts 2. On that day, the Holy Spirit was poured out on the disciples in a dramatic and powerful way. They were filled with the Spirit, and they began to speak in other tongues as the Spirit enabled them. This event marked the birth of the Church and the beginning of the disciples' mission to spread the Gospel to the ends of the earth.

The outpouring of the Holy Spirit at Pentecost was the fulfillment of Old Testament prophecies, such as Joel 2:28-29, which spoke of God's Spirit being poured out on all people. It also confirmed the promise that Jesus had made to His disciples. The Holy Spirit's coming empowered the disciples to preach boldly, perform miracles, and establish the early Christian community.

6.4 Preparing the Disciples for the Challenges Ahead

Jesus' promise of the Holy Spirit was not only about empowering the disciples for ministry but also about preparing them for the challenges and trials they would face. Jesus knew that after His departure, the disciples would encounter persecution, opposition, and moments of doubt. The Holy Spirit would be their source of strength, courage, and perseverance in the face of these difficulties.

6.4.1 The Reality of Persecution

In His final discourse, Jesus warned the disciples that they would face persecution because of their association with Him (John 15:18-20). The world would hate them, just as it hated Him. However, He assured them that the Holy Spirit would be with them, testifying to the truth of the Gospel and empowering them to stand firm in their faith (John 15:26-27).

The Holy Spirit's presence was crucial for the disciples as they faced persecution. It gave them the boldness to preach the Gospel fearlessly, even in the face of threats and violence. The book of Acts records numerous instances where the disciples, filled with the Holy Spirit, proclaimed the message of Christ with courage and conviction, despite the dangers they faced.

6.4.2 The Holy Spirit as Comforter

The Holy Spirit was also promised as a Comforter to the disciples. Jesus knew that His departure would bring sorrow and fear to His followers. They would feel abandoned and uncertain about the future. In response, Jesus promised that the Holy Spirit would come alongside them, providing comfort and assurance in times of distress.

The word "Comforter" (parakletos in Greek) carries the meaning of someone who is called to one's side to help, encourage, and support. The Holy Spirit would fulfill this role in the lives of the disciples, offering them peace and solace in the midst of trials. This comforting presence would remind them that they were not alone and that Jesus' love and care for them continued through the Spirit's work.

6.4.3 Empowerment for Mission

Finally, Jesus' promise of the Holy Spirit was directly connected to the mission that He had entrusted to the disciples. After His resurrection, Jesus commissioned the disciples to go into all the world and make disciples of all nations (Matthew 28:18-20). This Great Commission was a daunting task, one that would be impossible to accomplish in their own strength.

The Holy Spirit was given to empower the disciples for this mission. In Acts 1:8, Jesus told them, "But you shall receive power when the Holy Spirit has come upon you; and you shall be witnesses to Me in Jerusalem, and in all Judea and Samaria, and to the end of the earth." The Holy Spirit would provide the supernatural power needed to fulfill the mission, enabling the disciples to perform miracles, preach with authority, and endure persecution.

This empowerment was not just for the original disciples but for all believers throughout history. The same Holy Spirit who filled the disciples at Pentecost continues to empower Christians today to carry out the mission of spreading the Gospel and advancing God's Kingdom.

6.5 The Impact of the Holy Spirit on the Disciples' Lives and Ministry

The coming of the Holy Spirit had a transformative impact on the disciples' lives and ministry. Before Pentecost, the disciples were often portrayed as fearful, confused, and uncertain about their role in Jesus' mission. However, after the outpouring of the Holy Spirit, they were transformed into bold, confident, and effective witnesses for Christ.

6.5.1 Boldness in Proclamation

One of the most noticeable changes in the disciples after receiving the Holy Spirit was their boldness in proclaiming the Gospel. Peter, who had previously denied Jesus out of fear, stood up on the day of Pentecost and preached a powerful sermon that led to the conversion of three thousand people (Acts 2:14-41). The other disciples similarly displayed remarkable courage, preaching the Gospel openly and fearlessly, even in the face of threats and persecution.

6.5.2 Miraculous Signs and Wonders

The Holy Spirit also empowered the disciples to perform miraculous signs and wonders, confirming the truth of their message. In Acts 3, Peter and John healed a lame man at the temple gate, which led to an opportunity to preach the Gospel to the gathered crowd. Throughout the book of Acts, we see the disciples performing healings, casting out demons, and even raising the dead—all through the power of the Holy Spirit.

These miraculous acts were not just demonstrations of power but signs that pointed to the reality of God's Kingdom and the authority of Jesus Christ. They served to validate the disciples' message and to draw people to faith in Christ.

6.5.3 Establishing the Early Church

The Holy Spirit played a crucial role in the establishment and growth of the early Church. The disciples, guided and empowered by the Spirit, led the early Christian community, teaching, baptizing, and organizing the believers. The Holy Spirit also provided wisdom and guidance in addressing challenges and disputes within the Church, such as the issue of Gentile inclusion (Acts 15).

The early Church's rapid growth and the spread of the Gospel across the Roman Empire were direct results of the Holy Spirit's work in and through the disciples. The Spirit's presence unified the believers, enabled them to persevere through persecution, and inspired them to take the message of Christ to the ends of the earth.

6.6 Conclusion

The promise of the Holy Spirit was a central aspect of Jesus' preparation of His disciples for His departure. Knowing that His physical presence would no longer be with them, Jesus assured His followers that the Holy Spirit would come to guide, empower, and comfort them. This promise was fulfilled at Pentecost, marking the beginning of a new era in which the disciples were transformed by the Spirit's indwelling presence.

The impact of the Holy Spirit on the disciples' lives and ministry cannot be overstated. The Spirit provided them with the boldness, power, and guidance needed to fulfill the mission of spreading the Gospel and establishing the Church. The same Holy Spirit who empowered the disciples continues to work in the lives of believers today, guiding them into all truth, comforting them in times of trouble, and empowering them for mission.

As we reflect on Jesus' promise of the Holy Spirit, we are reminded that we, too, have access to this same Spirit. The Holy Spirit is our constant companion, teacher, and source of strength as we seek to follow Christ and fulfill the mission He has given us. The promise of the Holy Spirit is not just a historical event but a living reality that continues to shape the life of the Church and the faith of believers today.

CHAPTER 03

THE ROLE OF THE HOLY SPIRIT IN TESTIFYING TO JESUS' DIVINITY

The Paraclete: Who is the Holy Spirit, and What Does the Term Paraclete Mean?

7.1 Introduction

The Holy Spirit plays a vital role in the Christian understanding of God, particularly in the context of Jesus' ministry and His ongoing work in the world. One of the most profound ways Jesus described the Holy Spirit is through the term "Paraclete," a word rich in meaning and significance. Understanding who the Holy Spirit is and what the term Paraclete means is essential for grasping the Spirit's role in testifying to Jesus' divinity, empowering believers, and guiding the Church. In this chapter, we will explore the identity of the

Holy Spirit, the meaning of the term Paraclete, and the implications of this title for the life of faith.

7.2 Who Is the Holy Spirit?

Before delving into the meaning of the term Paraclete, it is important to establish who the Holy Spirit is within the framework of Christian theology. The Holy Spirit is the third person of the Holy Trinity, co-equal and co-eternal with God the Father and God the Son. The Spirit is not a mere force or impersonal power but a divine person who actively participates in the work of creation, redemption, and sanctification.

7.2.1 The Holy Spirit in the Old Testament

The presence and work of the Holy Spirit can be seen throughout the Old Testament. The Hebrew word for Spirit, "Ruach," refers to breath, wind, or spirit and is used to describe the creative power of God. In Genesis 1:2, the Spirit of God is depicted as hovering over the waters at the beginning of creation, bringing order out of chaos. The Spirit also empowered individuals for specific tasks, such as the judges, prophets, and kings of Israel. For example, the Spirit of the Lord came upon Samson, giving him supernatural strength (Judges 14:6), and the Spirit of the Lord anointed the prophets to speak God's word (Isaiah 61:1).

However, in the Old Testament, the Holy Spirit's presence was often temporary and selective, resting on certain individuals for specific purposes. The full and permanent indwelling of the Spirit in all believers, as promised by Jesus, was a reality that would only be realized in the New Testament era.

7.2.2 The Holy Spirit in the New Testament

In the New Testament, the Holy Spirit takes on a more prominent and personal role, particularly in the life and ministry of Jesus. The Spirit is intimately involved in the events of Jesus' life, from His conception (Luke 1:35) to His baptism (Matthew 3:16) and throughout His ministry. Jesus is described as being "full of the Holy Spirit" (Luke 4:1) and performing miracles "by the Spirit of God" (Matthew 12:28).

After Jesus' resurrection and ascension, the Holy Spirit is poured out on the disciples at Pentecost (Acts 2), marking the beginning of the Church's mission to the world. The New Testament reveals that the Holy Spirit is the one who regenerates believers (John 3:5), indwells them (1 Corinthians 3:16), and empowers them to live out the Christian life (Acts 1:8). The Spirit also plays a crucial role in revealing the truth about Jesus and guiding believers into all truth (John 16:13).

7.3 The Meaning of the Term Paraclete

The term "Paraclete" is one of the most significant titles given to the Holy Spirit in the New Testament. It is derived from the Greek word "parakletos," which appears primarily in the writings of John, particularly in the Gospel of John and the First Epistle of John. The term is difficult to translate into English because it carries a range of meanings, each of which sheds light on the multifaceted role of the Holy Spirit.

7.3.1 The Various Meanings of Paraclete

The word "Paraclete" can be translated in several ways, each capturing a different aspect of the Holy Spirit's work:

- Helper: One of the most common translations of Paraclete is "Helper." This translation emphasizes the Holy Spirit's role in assisting and supporting believers in their spiritual journey. The Holy Spirit is the one who comes alongside Christians to strengthen them in their faith, helping them to overcome challenges and to live in accordance with God's will.

- Comforter: Another translation of Paraclete is "Comforter." This interpretation highlights the Holy Spirit's role in providing solace and encouragement, particularly in times of distress or suffering. As the Comforter, the Holy

Spirit brings peace to troubled hearts and reassures believers of God's presence and love, even in difficult circumstances.

- Advocate: The term "Advocate" is another possible translation of Paraclete, drawing on a legal metaphor. In this sense, the Holy Spirit is seen as a legal advocate or defense attorney who represents believers before God and intercedes on their behalf. The Holy Spirit advocates for believers, defending them against the accusations of Satan and the condemnation of the world.

- Counselor: The word "Counselor" is also used to translate Paraclete, emphasizing the Holy Spirit's role in guiding and advising believers. As the Counselor, the Holy Spirit provides wisdom and insight, helping Christians to understand God's will and to make decisions that align with His purposes.

Each of these translations captures a different dimension of the Holy Spirit's work in the life of believers. Whether as Helper, Comforter, Advocate, or Counselor, the Holy Spirit is the one who comes alongside believers to support, guide, and empower them in their walk with God.

7.3.2 The Paraclete in the Gospel of John

The Gospel of John provides the most detailed description of the Holy Spirit as the Paraclete. In the farewell discourse (John 14-16), Jesus introduces the Paraclete to His disciples as the one who will take His place after His departure. Jesus reassures the disciples that even though He is leaving them, He will not leave them as orphans because the Paraclete will come to be with them forever (John 14:16-18).

In John 14:16-17, Jesus says, "And I will pray the Father, and He will give you another Helper, that He may abide with you forever—the Spirit of truth, whom the world cannot receive, because it neither sees Him nor knows Him; but you know Him, for He dwells with you and will be in you." This passage highlights several key aspects of the Paraclete's role:

- "Another Helper": The phrase "another Helper" implies that the Holy Spirit is of the same kind as Jesus. Just as Jesus has been the disciples' Helper, teaching, guiding, and protecting them, so the Holy Spirit will continue this role in Jesus' absence. The use of the word "another" suggests continuity and consistency in the way God cares for His people.

- "The Spirit of Truth": The Holy Spirit is described as the Spirit of truth, emphasizing His role in revealing and affirming the truth about Jesus and His teachings. The Spirit's work is to lead believers into a deeper understanding of the truth, helping them to discern what is right and to live according to God's will.

 - "He will be in you": Jesus promises that the Holy Spirit will not only be with the disciples but will be in them. This indwelling presence of the Spirit marks a profound change in the relationship between God and His people. The Holy Spirit's presence within believers signifies a new level of intimacy and empowerment, enabling them to live out the teachings of Jesus in their daily lives.

In John 15:26-27, Jesus further explains the Paraclete's role in bearing witness to Him: "But when the Helper comes, whom I shall send to you from the Father, the Spirit of truth who proceeds from the Father, He will testify of Me. And you also will bear witness, because you have been with Me from the beginning." Here, the Paraclete's work is directly connected to the mission of the disciples. The Holy Spirit will testify to the truth of Jesus' identity and mission, empowering the disciples to bear witness to Him as well.

In John 16:7-11, Jesus describes the Paraclete's work in the world: "Nevertheless I tell you the truth. It is to your advantage that I go away; for if I do not go away, the Helper will not come to you; but if I depart, I will send Him to you. And when He has come, He will convict the world of sin, and of righteousness, and of judgment: of sin, because they do not believe in Me; of righteousness, because I go to My Father and you see Me no more; of judgment, because the ruler of this world is judged." The Paraclete's work involves convicting the world of its need for salvation, revealing the righteousness of Christ, and declaring the victory over Satan and evil.

7.3.3 The Paraclete in 1 John

The term Paraclete also appears in the First Epistle of John, where it is used to describe Jesus Himself. In 1 John 2:1, the apostle writes, "My little children, these things I write to you, so that you may not sin. And if anyone sins, we have an Advocate with the Father, Jesus Christ the righteous." Here, Jesus is referred to as the Advocate (Paraclete) who intercedes on behalf of believers before the Father.

This dual application of the term Paraclete—referring to both Jesus and the Holy Spirit—highlights the unity and continuity of their work. Jesus, during His earthly ministry, was the Paraclete who guided, protected, and taught the disciples. After His ascension, the Holy Spirit took on this role, continuing Jesus' work in and through the lives of believers.

7.4 The Implications of the Paraclete for the Christian Life

The title Paraclete and the role of the Holy Spirit have profound implications for the Christian life. The Holy Spirit, as the Paraclete, is the one who enables believers to live out their faith in the midst of a challenging world. Understanding the Paraclete's role helps believers to rely on the Spirit's guidance, comfort, and power in every aspect of their lives.

7.4.1 The Holy Spirit as a Constant Companion

As the Paraclete, the Holy Spirit is the believer's constant companion. This presence is not limited to certain times or places but is an ongoing reality in the life of every Christian. The Holy Spirit's indwelling presence provides a continual source of strength, wisdom, and encouragement, enabling believers to face the trials and temptations of life with confidence.

7.4.2 The Holy Spirit as a Guide into Truth

The Holy Spirit's role as the Spirit of truth is essential for the believer's growth in understanding and applying God's Word. The Spirit illuminates the Scriptures, helping believers to grasp the depths of God's revelation and to discern His will. This guidance is especially important in a world filled with competing voices and ideologies. By relying on the Holy Spirit, believers can navigate the complexities of life with a clear sense of God's direction.

7.4.3 The Holy Spirit as an Empowerer for Mission

The Holy Spirit's empowerment is crucial for the believer's participation in God's mission. Just as the Spirit empowered the early disciples to preach the Gospel and establish the Church, so the Holy Spirit empowers believers today to carry out the Great Commission. The Spirit equips Christians with spiritual gifts, boldness, and a heart for service, enabling them to be effective witnesses for Christ in their communities and around the world.

7.4.4 The Holy Spirit as a Comforter in Times of Trial

In times of trial and suffering, the Holy Spirit's role as Comforter is especially precious. The Paraclete comes alongside believers, offering peace and reassurance when they are overwhelmed by life's challenges. This comfort is not just emotional support but a deep, spiritual assurance that God is present and working in every situation. The Holy Spirit reminds believers of God's promises and helps them to trust in His goodness, even in the darkest of times.

7.5 Conclusion

The term Paraclete, with its rich and varied meanings, offers a profound insight into the identity and work of the Holy Spirit. As Helper, Comforter, Advocate, and Counselor, the Holy Spirit plays a crucial role in the life of every believer, continuing the work that Jesus began during His earthly ministry. The Paraclete's presence and work are essential for understanding Jesus' divinity, for living out the Christian faith, and for fulfilling the mission of the Church.

As we reflect on the role of the Paraclete, we are reminded of the incredible gift that Jesus promised to His followers—the gift of the Holy Spirit. This gift is not just a theological concept but a living reality that empowers, guides, comforts, and sustains us in our walk with God. By embracing the work of the Holy Spirit in our lives, we can experience the fullness of God's presence and power, just as the disciples did, and continue the mission of making Jesus known to the world.

Guiding into All Truth: How the Holy Spirit Reveals the Truth About Jesus

8.1 Introduction

In John 16:13, Jesus promised His disciples that the Holy Spirit, whom He called the "Spirit of truth," would guide them into all truth. This promise was given in the context of Jesus' final discourse, where He was preparing His disciples for His imminent departure. The role of the Holy Spirit in revealing the truth about Jesus is central to the Christian faith, as it ensures that the teachings of Christ would be understood, preserved, and applied by His followers throughout the ages. In this chapter, we will explore how the Holy Spirit guides believers into all truth, with a particular focus on revealing the truth about Jesus—His identity, mission, and teachings.

8.2 The Context of John 16:13

To fully appreciate the significance of John 16:13, it is important to consider the broader context of Jesus' farewell discourse. As Jesus prepared to leave His disciples, He knew they would face a world filled with confusion, hostility, and spiritual challenges. Without His physical presence, the disciples might have felt abandoned and unsure of how to continue His mission.

In response to these concerns, Jesus reassured them by promising the Holy Spirit, who would come to guide them into all truth. He said, "However, when He, the Spirit of truth, has come, He will guide you into all truth; for He will not speak on His own authority, but whatever He hears He will speak; and He will tell you things to come" (John 16:13). This promise was meant to give the disciples confidence that they would not be left to navigate their faith journey alone. Instead, the Holy Spirit would be with them, leading them into a deeper understanding of Jesus and His teachings.

8.3 The Role of the Holy Spirit as the Spirit of Truth

The title "Spirit of truth" emphasizes the Holy Spirit's role in revealing and confirming the truth. Truth, in the biblical sense, is not just factual accuracy but is deeply connected to the nature and character of God. Jesus Himself declared, "I am the way, the truth, and the life" (John 14:6), indicating that truth is personified in Him. The Holy Spirit, therefore, is the one who leads believers into a fuller understanding of Jesus, who embodies the truth of God.

8.3.1 The Holy Spirit Reveals the Truth About Jesus' Identity

One of the primary ways the Holy Spirit guides believers into all truth is by revealing the truth about Jesus' identity. Throughout the Gospels, Jesus made claims about His divine nature, His relationship with the Father, and His role as the Savior of the world. However, the full implications of these claims were not always immediately clear to His disciples.

After Jesus' resurrection and the outpouring of the Holy Spirit at Pentecost, the disciples began to understand more fully who Jesus truly was. The Holy Spirit illuminated their minds, helping them to grasp the significance of Jesus' divinity, His fulfillment of Old Testament prophecies, and His unique role in God's plan of salvation.

For example, in Acts 2, we see Peter, filled with the Holy Spirit, boldly proclaiming that Jesus is both "Lord and Christ" (Acts 2:36). This proclamation reflects a deepened understanding of Jesus' identity, one that was made possible by the Holy Spirit's work in Peter's heart and mind. The Spirit revealed to Peter and the other disciples that Jesus was not just a great teacher or prophet, but the Son of God, the Messiah who had come to redeem humanity.

8.3.2 The Holy Spirit Illuminates Jesus' Teachings

Another crucial aspect of the Holy Spirit's role in guiding believers into all truth is the illumination of Jesus' teachings. During His ministry, Jesus taught many things that were challenging for His disciples to understand fully. He often spoke in parables and used metaphors that required deeper reflection to grasp.

The Holy Spirit helps believers to understand and apply these teachings in their lives. This process of illumination involves bringing to mind the words of Jesus, clarifying their meaning, and showing how they apply to specific situations. In John 14:26, Jesus said, "But the Helper, the Holy Spirit, whom the Father will send in My name, He will teach you all things, and bring to your remembrance all that I said to you."

This role of the Holy Spirit is particularly important in the context of studying Scripture. As believers read and meditate on the Bible, the Holy Spirit opens their understanding, helping them to see the relevance of Jesus' teachings for their lives. The Spirit also helps believers to see the continuity between the Old Testament and the New Testament, revealing how Jesus fulfills the promises and prophecies of the Scriptures.

8.3.3 The Holy Spirit Guides in the Interpretation of Scripture

The Holy Spirit's guidance is essential for the correct interpretation of Scripture. The Bible, while accessible to all, contains depths of meaning that require spiritual discernment to fully comprehend. The Holy Spirit provides this discernment, guiding believers into a proper understanding of God's Word.

The Apostle Paul emphasizes the importance of the Spirit in understanding spiritual truths. In 1 Corinthians 2:10-14, he writes, "But God has revealed them to us through His Spirit. For the Spirit searches all things, yes, the deep things of God... These things we also speak, not in words which man's wisdom teaches but which the Holy Spirit teaches, comparing spiritual things with spiritual. But the natural man does not receive the things of the Spirit of God, for they are foolishness to him; nor can he know them, because they are spiritually discerned."

This passage highlights that the truths of God are spiritually discerned and that it is the Holy Spirit who enables believers to understand them. Without the Spirit's guidance, even the most diligent study of Scripture could lead to misunderstandings or misinterpretations. The Spirit ensures that believers are led into a true and accurate understanding of God's Word, particularly as it relates to Jesus.

8.3.4 The Holy Spirit Testifies to Jesus' Work and Mission

The Holy Spirit also plays a vital role in testifying to the work and mission of Jesus. After Jesus' ascension, the Holy Spirit was sent to bear witness to Christ, empowering the disciples to continue His work. This testimony involves not only proclaiming the historical facts of Jesus' life, death, and resurrection but also revealing the spiritual significance of these events.

In John 15:26-27, Jesus said, "But when the Helper comes, whom I shall send to you from the Father, the Spirit of truth who proceeds from the Father, He will testify of Me. And you also will bear witness, because you have been with Me from the beginning." The Holy Spirit's testimony about Jesus is central to the Church's mission. The Spirit empowers believers to proclaim the Gospel, confirming the truth of Jesus' work through signs, wonders, and the transformation of lives.

The Holy Spirit's testimony also involves convicting the world of its need for Jesus. In John 16:8-11, Jesus explains that the Spirit will convict the world "of sin, and of righteousness, and of judgment: of sin, because they do not believe in Me; of righteousness, because I go to My Father and you see Me no more; of judgment, because the ruler of this world is judged." The Spirit's conviction leads people to recognize their need for salvation and to respond to the truth of the Gospel.

8.4 The Process of Being Guided Into All Truth

The Holy Spirit's guidance into all truth is not a one-time event but an ongoing process that occurs throughout the life of a believer. This process involves several key elements:

8.4.1 Continual Learning and Growth

The Christian life is one of continual learning and growth, and the Holy Spirit is the one who facilitates this process. As believers mature in their faith, the Holy Spirit leads them into deeper and fuller understandings of the truth. This growth is not merely intellectual but involves the whole person—mind, heart, and will.

The Spirit helps believers to apply the truths of Scripture to their daily lives, transforming their character and aligning their actions with God's will. This ongoing process of being guided into all truth is often referred to as sanctification, the work of the Holy Spirit in making believers more like Christ.

8.4.2 Discernment in a World of Deception

In a world where falsehoods and deceptions abound, the Holy Spirit's guidance is crucial for discerning truth from error. The Spirit helps believers to recognize and reject false teachings, philosophies, and ideologies that are contrary to the Gospel. In 1 John 4:1-3, the apostle John warns believers to "test the spirits" to see whether they are from God, and he provides the criterion for discernment: acknowledging Jesus Christ as having come in the flesh.

The Holy Spirit equips believers with the discernment needed to navigate a complex and often confusing world. This discernment is especially important in maintaining the purity of the Gospel and protecting the Church from false teachings that can lead people astray.

8.4.3 A Relationship of Trust and Dependence

Being guided into all truth by the Holy Spirit requires a relationship of trust and dependence on God. Believers must cultivate a posture of openness to the Spirit's leading, being willing to submit to His guidance even when it challenges their preconceived notions or requires difficult changes.

This relationship of trust is built through prayer, meditation on Scripture, and a willingness to listen to the Spirit's voice. As believers grow in their relationship with God, they become more attuned to the Holy Spirit's promptings and more confident in His ability to lead them into all truth.

8.4.4 The Role of the Community of Faith

While the Holy Spirit guides individual believers into all truth, this guidance often occurs within the context of the community of faith. The Church, as the body of Christ, is a place where the Holy Spirit works collectively to reveal the truth about Jesus. Through the teaching, preaching, and fellowship of the Church, the Holy Spirit helps believers to grow in their understanding of the truth.

The community of faith provides a space for believers to learn from one another, to test their understanding of Scripture, and to encourage one another in their walk with God. The Holy Spirit works through the Church to build up believers and to guide the entire community into a deeper understanding of God's truth.

8.5 The Implications of Being Guided Into All Truth

The Holy Spirit's work of guiding believers into all truth has profound implications for the Christian life:

8.5.1 Assurance of Faith

One of the key implications of being guided into all truth is the assurance of faith. The Holy Spirit confirms the truth of the Gospel in the hearts of believers, providing them with a deep and abiding confidence in their relationship with God. This assurance is not based on subjective feelings but on the objective work of the Spirit in revealing and affirming the truth about Jesus.

8.5.2 Empowerment for Witness

The Holy Spirit's guidance also empowers believers for witness. As believers are led into a deeper understanding of the truth about Jesus, they are equipped to share that truth with others. The Spirit provides the boldness, wisdom, and clarity needed to effectively communicate the Gospel and to bear witness to the reality of Jesus' life, death, and resurrection.

8.5.3 Transformation of Character

Being guided into all truth by the Holy Spirit results in the transformation of character. As believers grow in their understanding of Jesus and His teachings, the Holy Spirit works to conform them to the image of Christ. This transformation involves the development of the fruits of the

Spirit—love, joy, peace, patience, kindness, goodness, faithfulness, gentleness, and self-control (Galatians 5:22-23)—which reflect the character of Jesus in the life of the believer.

8.5.4 A Deeper Relationship with God

Finally, the Holy Spirit's guidance into all truth deepens the believer's relationship with God. As the Spirit reveals more about Jesus, believers come to know God more intimately and to experience His presence more fully. This deepening relationship is the heart of the Christian life, as believers are drawn closer to God through the work of the Holy Spirit.

8.6 Conclusion

The Holy Spirit's role in guiding believers into all truth is a central aspect of the Christian faith. As the Spirit of truth, the Holy Spirit reveals the truth about Jesus—His identity, mission, and teachings—ensuring that believers can understand, apply, and live out the Gospel in their lives. This guidance is an ongoing process that involves continual learning, discernment, trust, and community.

As we reflect on the Holy Spirit's work in guiding us into all truth, we are reminded of the incredible gift that Jesus promised to His followers. The Holy Spirit is not just a distant or abstract force but a personal and active presence in the life of every believer. By embracing the Spirit's guidance, we can grow in our understanding of Jesus, be empowered for witness, and experience the transformation that comes from living in the truth of the Gospel.

Convicting the World of Sin, Righteousness, and Judgment: The Role of the Holy Spirit in Leading People to Recognize Jesus as Divine

9.1 Introduction

In His farewell discourse, Jesus provided His disciples with a profound insight into the work of the Holy Spirit, particularly in relation to the world's recognition of His divinity. One of the central aspects of the Holy Spirit's role is to convict the world of sin, righteousness, and judgment. This conviction is not merely about moral or ethical awareness but is deeply connected to the revelation of Jesus Christ as the divine Son of God. In this chapter, we will explore how the Holy Spirit convicts the world of sin, righteousness, and judgment, and how this conviction leads people to recognize the divinity of Jesus.

9.2 Understanding the Holy Spirit's Role in Conviction

In John 16:8-11, Jesus describes the convicting work of the Holy Spirit: "And when He has come, He will convict the world of sin, and of righteousness, and of judgment: of sin, because they do not believe in Me; of righteousness, because I go to My Father and you see Me no more; of judgment, because the ruler of this world is judged." This passage outlines three areas in which the Holy Spirit convicts the world, each of which is intimately connected to the recognition of Jesus as divine.

9.2.1 Conviction as a Divine Work

Conviction, as described by Jesus, is a divine work that goes beyond human reasoning or persuasion. The Holy Spirit, as the third person of the Trinity, carries out this work by revealing the truth about Jesus to the hearts and minds of individuals. This conviction is an essential step in leading people to faith in Christ, as it confronts them with the reality of who Jesus is and what He has accomplished.

Conviction by the Holy Spirit is not simply about making people feel guilty for their sins. Rather, it is a profound spiritual awakening that opens their eyes to the truth of Jesus' identity and the implications of His life, death, and resurrection. Through this work, the Holy Spirit draws individuals to a point of decision, where they must either accept or reject the truth about Jesus.

9.3 Convicting the World of Sin

The first aspect of the Holy Spirit's convicting work is the conviction of sin. Jesus explains that the Holy Spirit convicts the world of sin "because they do not believe in Me" (John 16:9). This statement highlights the centrality of unbelief in the sin that the Holy Spirit exposes. At its core, sin is not merely a violation of moral laws but a rejection of Jesus Christ and His divine identity.

9.3.1 The Nature of Sin

In the biblical context, sin is fundamentally about the broken relationship between humanity and God. It is a rebellion against God's authority and a refusal to acknowledge His rightful place as Creator and Lord. This rebellion is most clearly manifested in humanity's rejection of Jesus, who is the fullest revelation of God to the world.

The Holy Spirit convicts people of their sin by revealing the truth about Jesus and showing them the gravity of their unbelief. This conviction involves an awareness of one's own guilt before God and the realization that rejecting Jesus is the most serious sin of all. As the Spirit reveals the holiness and righteousness of Jesus, individuals are confronted with their own sinfulness and their need for a Savior.

9.3.2 The Role of the Holy Spirit in Revealing Sin

The Holy Spirit reveals sin in a way that human effort cannot. While people may be aware of moral failings or ethical shortcomings, it is the Holy Spirit who brings to light the deeper issue of unbelief and rebellion against God. This revelation is not just an intellectual understanding but a deeply personal experience that penetrates the heart and soul.

In convicting the world of sin, the Holy Spirit also exposes the lies and deceptions that people use to justify their unbelief. The Spirit breaks through the hardness of heart and the blindness that prevents people from seeing the truth about Jesus. This work of conviction is essential for leading individuals to repentance and faith, as it brings them to the point where they recognize their need for forgiveness and the saving grace of Jesus Christ.

9.3.3 The Connection Between Sin and the Recognition of Jesus' Divinity

The conviction of sin is directly connected to the recognition of Jesus' divinity. When the Holy Spirit convicts individuals of their sin, He also reveals the true identity of Jesus as the Son of God. This revelation is crucial because it shows that sin is not just a violation of abstract principles but a personal offense against the divine Savior who gave His life to redeem humanity.

As people come to understand the seriousness of their sin, they are also led to recognize the divinity of Jesus, who alone has the power to forgive sins and restore the broken relationship between humanity and God. The Holy Spirit's conviction of sin, therefore, serves as a gateway to the acknowledgment of Jesus as Lord and Savior.

9.4 Convicting the World of Righteousness

The second aspect of the Holy Spirit's convicting work is the conviction of righteousness. Jesus explains that the Holy Spirit convicts the world of righteousness "because I go to My Father and you see Me no more" (John 16:10). This statement points to the righteousness of Jesus Himself and the vindication of His claims through His resurrection and ascension.

9.4.1 The Righteousness of Jesus

Righteousness, in the biblical sense, refers to the perfect moral and ethical standards of God. Jesus, as the incarnate Son of God, perfectly embodied this righteousness in His life and ministry. He lived a life of complete obedience to the Father, fulfilling the Law and the prophets, and demonstrating what true righteousness looks like.

However, the world rejected Jesus and accused Him of blasphemy, ultimately crucifying Him as a criminal. The Holy Spirit convicts the world of its error by revealing the truth about Jesus' righteousness, particularly through the events of His resurrection and ascension. These events serve as God's vindication of Jesus, proving that He is indeed the righteous Son of God.

9.4.2 The Role of the Holy Spirit in Revealing Righteousness

The Holy Spirit reveals the righteousness of Jesus by pointing to His resurrection and ascension as proof that He is who He claimed to be. The resurrection, in particular, is a powerful demonstration of Jesus' divine authority and righteousness. It shows that Jesus was not a mere human teacher or prophet but the Son of God who conquered sin and death.

Through the conviction of righteousness, the Holy Spirit also reveals the insufficiency of human righteousness. The world's standards of righteousness often fall short of God's perfect standard, and people tend to rely on their own efforts to justify themselves. The Holy Spirit exposes the inadequacy of self-righteousness and reveals that true righteousness can only be found in Jesus.

9.4.3 The Connection Between Righteousness and the Recognition of Jesus' Divinity

The conviction of righteousness is intimately connected to the recognition of Jesus' divinity. As the Holy

Spirit reveals the truth about Jesus' righteousness, He also leads people to see that Jesus is the divine Son of God, the only one who perfectly fulfills God's standards. This revelation is crucial because it shows that Jesus is not just an example to follow but the source of righteousness for all who believe in Him.

The Holy Spirit's work in convicting the world of righteousness leads to a deeper understanding of Jesus' role as the mediator between God and humanity. Through faith in Jesus, believers are clothed in His righteousness and are able to stand before God as justified and forgiven. This recognition of Jesus' divinity and righteousness is essential for salvation and for living a life that is pleasing to God.

9.5 Convicting the World of Judgment

The third aspect of the Holy Spirit's convicting work is the conviction of judgment. Jesus explains that the Holy Spirit convicts the world of judgment "because the ruler of this world is judged" (John 16:11). This statement refers to the judgment of Satan, the "ruler of this world," and the ultimate victory of Jesus over the forces of evil.

9.5.1 The Defeat of Satan

Satan, as the ruler of this world, represents the forces of darkness and rebellion against God. Throughout His ministry, Jesus confronted and overcame the power of Satan, culminating in His victory on the cross. The crucifixion, which appeared to be a defeat, was actually the means by which Jesus triumphed over sin, death, and Satan.

The resurrection of Jesus is the ultimate proof of Satan's defeat. By rising from the dead, Jesus demonstrated His power over death and secured the final judgment of Satan and all who follow him. The Holy Spirit convicts the world of this judgment, revealing that Satan's power has been broken and that Jesus is the rightful ruler of the world.

9.5.2 The Role of the Holy Spirit in Revealing Judgment

The Holy Spirit reveals the reality of judgment by making known the consequences of rejecting Jesus and aligning with the forces of evil. The conviction of judgment serves as a warning to the world that the time of grace and repentance is limited and that a final judgment is coming.

This conviction is not intended to induce fear but to lead people to recognize the seriousness of their choices and to turn to Jesus for salvation. The Holy Spirit's work in convicting the world of judgment underscores the reality of spiritual warfare and the importance of aligning oneself with Jesus, who has already won the victory.

9.5.3 The Connection Between Judgment and the Recognition of Jesus' Divinity

The conviction of judgment is closely tied to the recognition of Jesus' divinity. As the Holy Spirit reveals the truth about the judgment of Satan, He also reveals that Jesus is the divine judge who will ultimately bring justice to the world. Jesus' authority to judge is rooted in His divine identity as the Son of God, who has been given all authority in heaven and on earth (Matthew 28:18).

The recognition of Jesus as the divine judge is essential for understanding the full scope of His mission. Jesus is not only the Savior who offers forgiveness and righteousness but also the judge who will hold the world accountable for its response to Him. The Holy Spirit's conviction of judgment leads people to acknowledge Jesus' authority and to submit to Him as Lord.

9.6 The Transformative Impact of the Holy Spirit's Conviction

The convicting work of the Holy Spirit has a transformative impact on those who respond to it. As individuals are convicted of sin, righteousness, and judgment, they are led to a deeper understanding of Jesus' divinity and their need for Him as Savior and Lord.

9.6.1 Leading to Repentance and Faith

The Holy Spirit's conviction is the starting point for repentance and faith. As people are confronted with the reality of their sin and the righteousness of Jesus, they are moved to turn away from their old ways and to embrace the new life that Jesus offers. This repentance is not merely a change of behavior but a complete transformation of heart and mind, made possible by the Holy Spirit.

Faith in Jesus is the natural response to the Holy Spirit's conviction. When individuals recognize Jesus as the divine Son of God, they are compelled to trust in Him for their salvation. This faith is not based on human effort but on the revelation of Jesus' divinity and the work of the Holy Spirit in drawing people to Him.

9.6.2 Empowering for Righteous Living

The Holy Spirit's conviction also empowers believers to live righteously. As they are convicted of the righteousness of Jesus, they are inspired to pursue a life that reflects His character and values. The Holy Spirit works within believers to produce the fruit of righteousness, enabling them to live in a way that is pleasing to God.

This empowerment for righteous living is a testimony to the world of Jesus' divinity. As believers live out their faith in practical ways, they bear witness to the truth of Jesus and the transforming power of the Holy Spirit.

9.6.3 Bringing Assurance of Salvation

The Holy Spirit's work of conviction also brings assurance of salvation to believers. As they are convicted of sin, righteousness, and judgment, they come to a deeper understanding of their standing before God. The Holy Spirit assures them that their sins are forgiven, that they are clothed in the righteousness of Jesus, and that they are safe from the judgment that is to come.

This assurance is a source of peace and confidence for believers as they navigate the challenges of life. It also strengthens their faith and encourages them to continue growing in their relationship with Jesus.

9.7 Conclusion

The Holy Spirit's work of convicting the world of sin, righteousness, and judgment is a vital part of leading people to recognize Jesus as divine. Through this conviction, the Holy Spirit reveals the truth about Jesus' identity, His righteousness, and His authority as the divine judge. This revelation is essential for bringing people to repentance, faith, and a transformed life in Christ.

As we reflect on the Holy Spirit's convicting work, we are reminded of the importance of responding to His leading with humility and openness. The Holy Spirit's conviction is not meant to condemn but to draw us closer to Jesus, the one who offers forgiveness, righteousness, and eternal life. By embracing the truth revealed by the Holy Spirit, we can grow in our understanding of Jesus' divinity and live out our faith with confidence and assurance.

CHAPTER 04

JESUS' PROPHECTIC ROLE

Foretelling the Future: Jesus' Predictions About His Death and Resurrection

10.1 Introduction

One of the most significant aspects of Jesus' prophetic role was His ability to foretell the future, particularly regarding His own death and resurrection. These predictions were not merely displays of foreknowledge but were central to His mission as the Messiah. Jesus' repeated and precise predictions about His death and resurrection reveal His awareness of His divine purpose and underscore His authority as the Son of God. In this chapter, we will explore the key instances where Jesus predicted His death and resurrection, the reactions of His disciples, and the theological implications of these predictions.

10.2 The First Prediction: The Turning Point at Caesarea Philippi

The first explicit prediction of Jesus' death and resurrection is recorded in the Synoptic Gospels (Matthew 16:21-23, Mark 8:31-33, Luke 9:22). This prediction occurred shortly after Peter's confession that Jesus is the Christ, the Son of the living God, at Caesarea Philippi.

10.2.1 The Context of the Prediction

The context of this first prediction is crucial. Jesus had just been identified by Peter as the Messiah, a confession that marked a turning point in His ministry. However, the disciples' understanding of the Messiah was influenced by Jewish expectations of a conquering king who would liberate Israel from Roman rule. Jesus, aware of their misconceptions, sought to correct their understanding by revealing the true nature of His messianic mission.

10.2.2 The Content of the Prediction

Jesus told His disciples, "The Son of Man must suffer many things, and be rejected by the elders and chief priests and scribes, and be killed, and after three days rise again" (Mark 8:31). This prediction was shocking to the disciples, who had not anticipated that the Messiah would suffer and die. Jesus used the title "Son of Man," which carries both a messianic and a human connotation, emphasizing His role as the representative of humanity who would suffer on their behalf.

The use of the word "must" indicates that Jesus' suffering and death were necessary and ordained by God. This was not a tragic accident but the fulfillment of divine purpose. The prediction also includes the promise of resurrection, which would vindicate Jesus and demonstrate His victory over death.

10.2.3 The Disciples' Reaction

Peter, unable to reconcile the idea of a suffering Messiah with his expectations, rebuked Jesus, saying, "Far be it from You, Lord; this shall not happen to You!" (Matthew 16:22). Jesus responded sternly, "Get behind Me, Satan! You are an offense to Me, for you are not mindful of the things of God, but the things of men" (Matthew 16:23). This exchange highlights the tension between human expectations and divine purpose. Peter's reaction reflects a common human tendency to resist the idea of suffering and sacrifice, particularly when it involves someone as revered as the Messiah.

Jesus' rebuke of Peter is significant because it underscores the importance of submitting to God's plan, even when it contradicts human desires or understanding. Jesus knew that His death and resurrection were the central events in God's redemptive plan, and He was resolutely committed to fulfilling His mission.

10.3 The Second Prediction: Reinforcing the Message

Following the first prediction, Jesus continued to teach His disciples about His impending death and resurrection. The second prediction, recorded in all three Synoptic Gospels (Matthew 17:22-23, Mark 9:30-32, Luke 9:43-45), occurred after the Transfiguration, where Peter, James, and John witnessed Jesus in His glorified state alongside Moses and Elijah.

10.3.1 The Context of the Prediction

The Transfiguration was a moment of divine revelation, affirming Jesus' identity as the Son of God and giving the disciples a glimpse of His future glory. However, immediately after this event, Jesus again spoke of His death, reminding the disciples that His path to glory would pass through suffering.

10.3.2 The Content of the Prediction

Jesus said to His disciples, "The Son of Man is about to be betrayed into the hands of men, and they will kill Him. And after He is killed, He will rise the third day" (Mark 9:31). This prediction adds the element of betrayal, indicating that Jesus would be handed over to His enemies by someone close to Him. The inevitability of His death and the promise of resurrection are once again emphasized.

10.3.3 The Disciples' Reaction

The disciples' reaction to this second prediction was one of confusion and fear. Mark records that they did not understand the saying and were afraid to ask Him (Mark 9:32). Luke adds that the meaning of Jesus' words was hidden from them (Luke 9:45). The disciples struggled to comprehend the idea that their Messiah, who had demonstrated such divine power and authority, would suffer and die. Their fear and confusion likely stemmed from the apparent contradiction between Jesus' predictions and their hopes for a triumphant, earthly kingdom.

This reaction reveals the limitations of human understanding when faced with the mysteries of God's plan. The disciples were on a journey of discovery, and it would take time—and the events of the crucifixion and resurrection—for them to fully grasp the significance of Jesus' words.

10.4 The Third Prediction: Emphasizing the Certainty of His Death and Resurrection

The third prediction of Jesus' death and resurrection is recorded in Matthew 20:17-19, Mark 10:32-34, and Luke 18:31-34. This prediction occurred as Jesus and His disciples were on their way to Jerusalem, where the final events of His earthly ministry would unfold.

10.4.1 The Context of the Prediction

As Jesus approached Jerusalem, the tension and anticipation among the disciples grew. They knew that Jerusalem was the center of religious and political power in Israel, and they likely expected that something significant would happen there. Jesus, aware of their expectations and the events that awaited Him, took the opportunity to speak to them more explicitly about what was to come.

10.4.2 The Content of the Prediction

Jesus took the twelve disciples aside and said, "Behold, we are going up to Jerusalem, and the Son of Man will be betrayed to the chief priests and to the scribes; and they will condemn Him to death, and deliver Him to the Gentiles to mock and to scourge and to crucify. And the third day He will rise again" (Matthew 20:18-19).

This prediction is the most detailed of the three, specifying the manner of Jesus' death—crucifixion—and the involvement of both Jewish and Gentile authorities. Jesus' reference to crucifixion, a form of execution reserved for the worst criminals, would have been shocking to the disciples. The prediction also reiterates the certainty of His resurrection, underscoring that His death would not be the end but the prelude to His victory over sin and death.

10.4.3 The Disciples' Reaction

The Gospels do not record an immediate verbal reaction from the disciples to this third prediction, but the context suggests that they were still struggling to come to terms with what Jesus was saying. Luke notes that the disciples "understood none of these things; this saying was hidden from them, and they did not know the things which were spoken" (Luke 18:34). This lack of understanding indicates that the full significance of Jesus' words was still beyond their grasp.

The disciples' inability to fully comprehend these predictions is understandable, given the radical nature of what Jesus was foretelling. The idea that the Messiah would suffer and die, let alone rise from the dead, was contrary to their expectations and to the prevailing Jewish beliefs of the time. It was only after the resurrection that they would fully understand and appreciate the prophetic nature of Jesus' predictions.

10.5 The Fulfillment of the Predictions

The fulfillment of Jesus' predictions about His death and resurrection is recorded in the Gospels' accounts of the Passion and Easter events. These events confirm the accuracy of Jesus' prophetic words and reveal the divine purpose behind His suffering.

10.5.1 The Passion: Suffering and Death

The Gospels describe in detail the events leading up to Jesus' crucifixion, including His betrayal by Judas, His trials before the Jewish and Roman authorities, the mockery and scourging He endured, and finally, His crucifixion. Each of these events fulfilled the predictions Jesus had made, demonstrating that His death was not a tragic accident but the fulfillment of God's plan for the redemption of humanity.

The crucifixion, while a moment of intense suffering and apparent defeat, was in fact the climax of Jesus' mission. Through His death, Jesus took upon Himself the sins of the world, offering Himself as the perfect sacrifice for sin. His cry from the cross, "It is finished" (John 19:30), signaled the completion of His redemptive work.

10.5.2 The Resurrection: Victory Over Death

On the third day after His crucifixion, Jesus rose from the dead, just as He had predicted. The resurrection is the ultimate vindication of Jesus' claims and the definitive proof of His divinity. It demonstrates His power over death and confirms that He is the Son of God, the promised Messiah.

The resurrection appearances of Jesus to His disciples and other followers further solidify the truth of His predictions. These appearances transformed the disciples from a group of frightened, disheartened followers into bold proclaimers of the Gospel. The resurrection became the central message of the early Christian Church, a message that continues to be proclaimed to this day.

10.6 The Theological Significance of Jesus' Predictions

Jesus' predictions about His death and resurrection are not only remarkable for their accuracy but also for their profound theological significance. They reveal key aspects of Jesus' identity, mission, and the nature of God's redemptive plan.

10.6.1 Jesus as the Fulfillment of Prophecy

By predicting His own death and resurrection, Jesus positioned Himself as the fulfillment of Old Testament prophecies concerning the Messiah. His suffering, death, and resurrection were in accordance with the Scriptures, fulfilling the words of the prophets. For example, Isaiah 53 speaks of the suffering servant who would be "pierced for our transgressions" and "crushed for our iniquities," a prophecy that finds its fulfillment in Jesus.

10.6.2 The Necessity of the Cross

Jesus' predictions highlight the necessity of the cross in God's plan of salvation. The cross was not an optional or accidental event but the central act of God's redemptive work. Through His death, Jesus paid the penalty for sin, satisfying the demands of God's justice and opening the way for humanity to be reconciled to God.

10.6.3 The Assurance of the Resurrection

The resurrection of Jesus is the cornerstone of Christian faith. It is the assurance that death has been conquered, that sin has been defeated, and that eternal life is available to all who believe in Him. Jesus' predictions about His resurrection underscore the certainty of this hope, providing believers with the confidence that their faith is grounded in the reality of a risen Savior.

10.6.4 The Authority of Jesus

Jesus' ability to predict His death and resurrection with such precision is a powerful testimony to His divine authority. It shows that He was in complete control of the events leading up to His crucifixion and that He willingly laid down His life for the sake of humanity. His predictions also affirm His identity as the Son of God, who has the power to lay down His life and to take it up again (John 10:18).

10.7 The Disciples' Post-Resurrection Understanding

After the resurrection, the disciples' understanding of Jesus' predictions was transformed. The events that had once been shrouded in mystery and confusion now became clear.

The Holy Spirit, whom Jesus had promised, opened their minds to understand the Scriptures and the significance of His death and resurrection (Luke 24:45).

10.7.1 The Role of the Holy Spirit

The Holy Spirit played a crucial role in helping the disciples to grasp the full meaning of Jesus' predictions. On the day of Pentecost, the Spirit empowered the disciples to proclaim the Gospel with boldness, testifying to the truth of Jesus' death and resurrection. Peter's sermon in Acts 2 is a prime example of this transformation, as he boldly declares that Jesus is the Messiah who was crucified and raised from the dead in fulfillment of God's plan.

10.7.2 The Formation of Christian Doctrine

The resurrection also became the foundation of Christian doctrine. The apostles and early Church fathers based their teachings on the reality of the resurrection, which validated everything that Jesus had said and done. The predictions of Jesus about His death and resurrection were central to the development of key Christian doctrines, including the atonement, justification by faith, and the hope of eternal life.

10.7.3 The Spread of the Gospel

The certainty of Jesus' predictions and their fulfillment fueled the spread of the Gospel throughout the Roman

Empire and beyond. The apostles' conviction that Jesus had risen from the dead and that His resurrection was the guarantee of eternal life gave them the courage to face persecution, imprisonment, and even death. The message of the crucified and risen Christ became the driving force behind the missionary efforts of the early Church, leading to the establishment of Christian communities across the known world.

10.8 Conclusion

Jesus' predictions about His death and resurrection are among the most remarkable aspects of His prophetic role. These predictions not only demonstrate His foreknowledge and authority but also reveal the centrality of the cross and resurrection in God's redemptive plan. Through His death, Jesus accomplished the work of salvation, and through His resurrection, He confirmed His identity as the divine Son of God and the Savior of the world.

The fulfillment of these predictions serves as a powerful testimony to the truth of the Christian faith and provides believers with the assurance that their hope is grounded in the reality of a risen Lord. As we reflect on these predictions, we are reminded of the depth of God's love for humanity, the necessity of the cross, and the certainty of the resurrection. These truths continue to inspire and sustain the faith of believers as they live in the light of Jesus' victory over sin and death.

Prophet Greater Than Moses: Jesus Fulfilling the Role of the Ultimate Prophet

11.1 Introduction

Throughout the Bible, Moses is revered as one of the greatest prophets in Israel's history. He was the mediator of the Old Covenant, the leader who delivered Israel from slavery in Egypt, and the one through whom God gave the Law. However, the Old Testament also foretold the coming of a prophet greater than Moses, one who would fulfill and surpass the role that Moses played in God's redemptive plan. In the New Testament, this ultimate prophet is revealed to be Jesus Christ. In this chapter, we will explore how Jesus fulfills and exceeds the role of Moses as the ultimate prophet, examining the parallels and contrasts between the two and the significance of this fulfillment for the Christian faith.

11.2 Moses: The Prototype of the Prophet

To understand how Jesus fulfills the role of the ultimate prophet, it is essential to first consider the role of Moses in the biblical narrative. Moses was not only a prophet but also a lawgiver, leader, and mediator between God and the people of Israel. His life and ministry set the pattern for what it meant to be a prophet in Israel.

11.2.1 Moses as the Mediator of the Covenant

Moses is most famously known for his role in delivering the Israelites from slavery in Egypt. Through Moses, God performed miraculous signs and wonders, culminating in the Passover and the parting of the Red Sea. These events were foundational to Israel's identity as God's chosen people.

Moses also served as the mediator of the Old Covenant. At Mount Sinai, he received the Law from God, which included the Ten Commandments and the detailed instructions for worship and community life. Moses then communicated these divine instructions to the people of Israel, establishing the covenant relationship between God and His people. In this role, Moses acted as a bridge between God and Israel, bringing God's words to the people and interceding on their behalf.

11.2.2 The Prophetic Role of Moses

In addition to being a lawgiver and leader, Moses was a prophet. He spoke God's words to the people, delivered God's judgments, and foretold future events, including blessings for obedience and curses for disobedience. Moses' prophetic ministry was marked by a unique intimacy with

God, as described in Numbers 12:6-8: "When a prophet of the Lord is among you, I reveal myself to him in visions, I speak to him in dreams. But this is not true of my servant Moses; he is faithful in all my house. With him, I speak face to face, clearly and not in riddles; he sees the form of the Lord."

Moses' close relationship with God set him apart from other prophets and established him as the prototype of the prophetic office in Israel. However, Moses himself anticipated the coming of a greater prophet, as recorded in Deuteronomy 18:15-18: "The Lord your God will raise up for you a prophet like me from among your own brothers. You must listen to him. For this is what you asked of the Lord your God at Horeb on the day of the assembly when you said, 'Let us not hear the voice of the Lord our God nor see this great fire anymore, or we will die.' The Lord said to me: 'What they say is good. I will raise up for them a prophet like you from among their brothers; I will put my words in his mouth, and he will tell them everything I command him.'"

11.3 The Promise of a Greater Prophet

The promise of a prophet like Moses, who would come to lead God's people and speak God's words, was a significant part of Israel's messianic expectation. The people of Israel understood that this prophet would not only resemble Moses but would also bring about a new and greater revelation of God's will.

11.3.1 The Anticipation of the Messiah

Throughout the Old Testament, there were many prophets, but none fully matched the role of Moses. The expectation of a coming prophet who would be like Moses became intertwined with the messianic hope for a deliverer who would restore Israel and establish God's kingdom. The Jewish people longed for the fulfillment of this promise, looking forward to the day when God would raise up this ultimate prophet.

By the time of Jesus, this expectation was still very much alive. When John the Baptist began his ministry, some people wondered if he might be the prophet like Moses (John 1:21). However, John denied that he was the prophet and pointed instead to the coming of one greater than himself, whose sandals he was not worthy to untie (John 1:27).

11.3.2 Jesus as the Fulfillment of the Promise

In the New Testament, Jesus is revealed as the fulfillment of the promise of a prophet like Moses. This fulfillment is not just in the sense of a continuation of Moses' ministry but as one who surpasses Moses in every way. Jesus is not merely a prophet among prophets; He is the ultimate prophet, the very Word of God made flesh (John 1:14).

Throughout His ministry, Jesus demonstrated that He was the prophet greater than Moses. He spoke with divine authority, performed miracles that surpassed those of Moses, and revealed the fullness of God's will. In the Sermon on the Mount (Matthew 5-7), Jesus spoke as one who had the authority to interpret and even expand upon the Law given through Moses, saying, "You have heard that it was said... But I tell you..." (Matthew 5:21-22, 27-28, 31-32, 33-34, 38-39, 43-44).

11.4 Jesus and Moses: Parallels and Contrasts

To fully appreciate how Jesus fulfills the role of the ultimate prophet, it is helpful to examine the parallels and contrasts between Jesus and Moses. These comparisons highlight both the continuity and the superiority of Jesus' ministry.

11.4.1 Parallels Between Jesus and Moses

- Miraculous Births: Both Moses and Jesus were born under miraculous circumstances. Moses was born during a time of oppression in Egypt, and his life was miraculously preserved when he was placed in a basket on the Nile River. Similarly, Jesus was born of a virgin, fulfilling the prophecy of Isaiah 7:14, and His birth was marked by angelic announcements and divine protection from King Herod's attempt to kill Him.

- Deliverance of God's People: Moses is most famous for leading the Israelites out of slavery in Egypt, an event that became central to Israel's identity and worship. Jesus, in a greater way, delivers God's people from the bondage of sin and death through His death and resurrection. Whereas Moses led a physical exodus, Jesus leads a spiritual exodus, bringing people into the freedom of the kingdom of God.

- Mediators of Covenants: Moses was the mediator of the Old Covenant, which was based on the Law given at Sinai. Jesus, by contrast, is the mediator of the New Covenant, established through His blood (Luke 22:20). The New Covenant surpasses the Old, as it is based on grace and truth, providing a way for all people to enter into a relationship with God.

- Lawgivers and Teachers: Moses received and delivered the Law of God to Israel, teaching them how to live as God's covenant people. Jesus, however, is the embodiment of God's Law and the ultimate teacher, who not only explains the Law but fulfills it perfectly (Matthew 5:17). In Jesus, the fullness of God's moral and ethical will is revealed.

11.4.2 Contrasts Between Jesus and Moses

- Divine Nature: While Moses was a great prophet and servant of God, he was still a human being with limitations. Jesus, on the other hand, is not only fully human but also fully divine. He is the Son of God, co-equal with the Father, and the exact representation of God's being (Hebrews 1:3). This divine nature sets Jesus apart as greater than any prophet, including Moses.

- Intimacy with God: Moses had an unparalleled relationship with God, speaking with Him "face to face" (Numbers 12:8). However, Jesus has an even greater intimacy with the Father, as He is eternally one with the Father (John 10:30). Jesus does not merely speak with God; He speaks as God, revealing the Father to the world (John 14:9).

- The Nature of Revelation: The revelation given through Moses was partial and preparatory, pointing forward to the greater revelation that would come through Jesus. The Law given through Moses served to guide and convict, but it was limited in its ability to transform hearts. Jesus, as the ultimate prophet, brings the fullness of God's revelation, offering not just guidance but also the power to transform lives through the Holy Spirit.

- The Scope of Salvation: Moses' mission was focused on the nation of Israel, leading them out of Egypt and establishing them as God's covenant people. Jesus' mission, however, is global in scope. He came to bring salvation to all people, Jew and Gentile alike, fulfilling God's promise to bless all nations through Abraham's offspring (Genesis 12:3; Galatians 3:8).

11.5 Jesus as the Ultimate Prophet in the New Testament

The New Testament writers consistently present Jesus as the fulfillment of the promise of a prophet like Moses, but also as someone who surpasses Moses in every way.

11.5.1 The Transfiguration

One of the most significant New Testament events that highlights Jesus' superiority over Moses is the Transfiguration. In this event, recorded in Matthew 17:1-8, Mark 9:2-8, and Luke 9:28-36, Jesus is revealed in His divine glory on a mountain, with Moses and Elijah appearing beside Him. Peter, James, and John witness this event, and Peter suggests building three shelters for Jesus, Moses, and Elijah.

However, a voice from heaven interrupts, saying, "This is My beloved Son, in whom I am well pleased. Hear Him!" (Matthew 17:5). This divine affirmation makes it clear that Jesus is not just another prophet like Moses or Elijah but is the Son of God, whose words must be heeded above all others. The Transfiguration underscores Jesus' unique status as the ultimate prophet and the fulfillment of all that Moses and Elijah represented.

11.5.2 The Book of Hebrews

The book of Hebrews also emphasizes the superiority of Jesus over Moses. The author writes, "Therefore, holy brethren, partakers of the heavenly calling, consider the Apostle and High Priest of our confession, Christ Jesus, who was faithful to Him who appointed Him, as Moses also was faithful in all His house. For this One has been counted worthy of more glory than Moses, inasmuch as He who built the house has more honor than the house" (Hebrews 3:1-3).

Hebrews presents Jesus as the builder of God's house, while Moses is a servant within that house. This imagery illustrates the difference in status between the two: Moses was a faithful servant, but Jesus is the Son and the builder, worthy of greater honor and glory.

11.5.3 The Acts of the Apostles

In the book of Acts, the early Christian community continues to identify Jesus as the prophet like Moses. In Acts 3:22-23, Peter quotes Deuteronomy 18:15 and applies it to Jesus, urging the people to listen to Him: "For Moses truly said to the fathers, 'The Lord your God will raise up for you a Prophet like me from your brethren. Him you shall hear in all things, whatever He says to you. And it shall be that every soul who will not hear that Prophet shall be utterly destroyed from among the people.'"

Peter's use of this passage underscores the importance of recognizing Jesus as the fulfillment of the prophecy. Those who reject Jesus are rejecting the ultimate revelation of God and are placing themselves outside of God's covenant promises.

11.6 The Significance of Jesus as the Ultimate Prophet

Jesus' role as the ultimate prophet has profound implications for Christian faith and life. His fulfillment of the role of prophet greater than Moses shapes our understanding of who He is, how we relate to God, and how we live out our faith.

11.6.1 The Authority of Jesus' Teachings

As the ultimate prophet, Jesus' teachings carry divine authority. When we read the Gospels and the teachings of Jesus, we are not just encountering the words of a wise teacher or moral leader; we are hearing the very words of God. This demands a response of obedience and submission to His authority. Jesus' teachings are not optional advice but the commands of the one who has all authority in heaven and on earth (Matthew 28:18).

11.6.2 The Finality of Revelation in Christ

Jesus' fulfillment of the prophetic role means that He is the final and ultimate revelation of God. In the past, God spoke through the prophets at various times and in various ways, but in these last days, He has spoken to us by His Son (Hebrews 1:1-2). This means that in Jesus, we have the complete and final word from God. While God continues to speak through His Spirit and through Scripture, all revelation is centered on and must be understood in light of Jesus Christ.

11.6.3 The Call to Listen and Obey

The voice from heaven at the Transfiguration commands us to "hear Him!" This call to listen to Jesus is central to the Christian life. To listen to Jesus means to accept His teachings, to follow His example, and to live according to His commands. It means allowing His words to shape our beliefs, values, and actions. As the ultimate prophet, Jesus calls us to a life of discipleship, where we continually seek to hear and obey His voice.

11.6.4 The Global Mission of the Church

Jesus' role as the ultimate prophet also has implications for the mission of the Church. Just as Moses led the Israelites out of Egypt, Jesus calls the Church to lead people out of spiritual bondage and into the freedom of God's kingdom. The Great Commission (Matthew 28:18-20) is the Church's mandate to proclaim the teachings of Jesus to all nations, making disciples and teaching them to obey everything He has commanded. As the Church carries out this mission, it bears witness to the truth that Jesus is the ultimate prophet, the one through whom God has revealed His will to the world.

11.7 Conclusion

Jesus' fulfillment of the role of the ultimate prophet greater than Moses is a central theme in the New Testament and a foundational truth of the Christian faith. As the prophet greater than Moses, Jesus brings the final and complete revelation of God's will, embodies the fullness of God's righteousness, and offers the ultimate deliverance from sin and death. His teachings carry divine authority, His life reveals the character of God, and His death and resurrection secure the salvation of all who believe in Him.

As we reflect on Jesus as the ultimate prophet, we are called to listen to His voice, to follow His example, and to proclaim His message to the world. In doing so, we participate in the ongoing fulfillment of God's redemptive plan, bearing witness to the truth that in Jesus, all the promises of God find their "Yes" and "Amen" (2 Corinthians 1:20). Jesus is not only the prophet like Moses; He is the one who surpasses all others, the Son of God, the Savior of the world, and the Lord of all creation.

The Holy Spirit as the Continuation of Jesus' Prophetic Work: How the Holy Spirit Continues Jesus' Work on Earth

12.1 Introduction

When Jesus ascended into heaven, His physical presence on Earth came to an end, but His work did not. He promised His disciples that He would send the Holy Spirit, who would not only be with them but would also continue the work that Jesus had begun. The Holy Spirit plays a crucial role in the ongoing mission of the Church, serving as the continuation of Jesus' prophetic work on Earth. In this chapter, we will explore how the Holy Spirit continues Jesus' work, focusing on the ways in which the Spirit teaches, guides, empowers, and comforts believers, ensuring that Jesus' mission is carried forward in the world.

12.2 The Promise of the Holy Spirit

Before His crucifixion, Jesus made several promises about the coming of the Holy Spirit. He assured His disciples that the Spirit would be their Helper, guiding them into all truth and reminding them of everything He had taught them (John 14:26; 16:13). This promise was fulfilled at Pentecost, when the Holy Spirit was poured out on the disciples, marking the beginning of the Spirit's work in continuing Jesus' prophetic ministry.

12.2.1 The Holy Spirit as the Paraclete

The Greek word "Paraclete," often translated as "Helper," "Comforter," or "Advocate," captures the essence of the Holy Spirit's role in the life of the Church. The Holy Spirit is the one who comes alongside believers to support, guide, and empower them in their walk with God. As the continuation of Jesus' prophetic work, the Holy Spirit takes on the role of the Paraclete, ensuring that the teachings and mission of Jesus are carried forward.

12.2.2 The Outpouring of the Holy Spirit at Pentecost

The day of Pentecost, as described in Acts 2, was a pivotal moment in the history of the Church. The Holy Spirit descended upon the disciples, filling them with power and enabling them to speak in various languages. This event marked the official beginning of the Church's mission to proclaim the Gospel to all nations.

Pentecost also demonstrated that the Holy Spirit was not just a temporary presence but a permanent indwelling in the lives of believers. The Spirit's presence signified that Jesus' work would continue through His followers, empowered and guided by the Holy Spirit.

12.3 The Teaching and Guiding Work of the Holy Spirit

One of the primary ways the Holy Spirit continues Jesus' prophetic work is through teaching and guiding believers. Just as Jesus taught His disciples during His earthly ministry, the Holy Spirit teaches and guides believers into a deeper understanding of God's truth.

12.3.1 The Spirit of Truth

In John 16:13, Jesus referred to the Holy Spirit as the "Spirit of truth," emphasizing the Spirit's role in leading believers into all truth. The Holy Spirit reveals the truth about God, Jesus, and the Scriptures, helping believers to grow in their knowledge and understanding of the faith. This teaching work of the Holy Spirit is a continuation of Jesus' own teaching, ensuring that the Church remains rooted in the truth of the Gospel.

The Holy Spirit also helps believers to discern the truth in a world filled with conflicting messages and false teachings. By illuminating the Scriptures and giving spiritual insight, the Holy Spirit enables believers to recognize and hold fast to the truth.

12.3.2 Reminding Believers of Jesus' Teachings

Another important aspect of the Holy Spirit's work is to remind believers of everything Jesus taught. In John 14:26, Jesus said, "But the Helper, the Holy Spirit, whom the Father will send in My name, He will teach you all things, and bring to your remembrance all things that I said to you."

This role of the Holy Spirit is particularly important in the context of the early Church, where the apostles and other believers needed to recall and accurately transmit the teachings of Jesus. The Spirit ensured that the message of Jesus was preserved and passed down through the generations, ultimately resulting in the New Testament writings.

Today, the Holy Spirit continues this work by helping believers to remember and apply the teachings of Jesus in their daily lives. The Spirit brings to mind the words of Jesus at the right moments, providing guidance, comfort, and conviction.

12.3.3 Leading into New Understandings

While the Holy Spirit reminds believers of what Jesus taught, the Spirit also leads them into new understandings of God's will and purpose. This does not mean that the Spirit introduces new doctrines but rather that the Spirit helps believers to apply the timeless truths of the Gospel to new situations and challenges.

Throughout the history of the Church, the Holy Spirit has guided believers in understanding how the teachings of Jesus apply to different cultural, social, and ethical issues. This ongoing work of the Spirit ensures that the Church remains relevant and faithful to its mission in every age.

12.4 The Empowering Work of the Holy Spirit

In addition to teaching and guiding, the Holy Spirit empowers believers to carry out the mission of Jesus. Just as Jesus performed His ministry in the power of the Holy Spirit, so too are believers called to continue His work in the world through the Spirit's empowerment.

12.4.1 Empowerment for Witness

One of the most significant ways the Holy Spirit empowers believers is for witness. In Acts 1:8, Jesus told His disciples, "But you shall receive power when the Holy Spirit has come upon you; and you shall be witnesses to Me in Jerusalem, and in all Judea and Samaria, and to the end of the earth."

The Holy Spirit empowers believers to boldly proclaim the Gospel and to bear witness to the truth of Jesus' death and resurrection. This empowerment is not limited to words alone but is also demonstrated through the lives of believers, who reflect the character of Christ in their actions and relationships.

12.4.2 The Gifts of the Spirit

The Holy Spirit also empowers believers through the distribution of spiritual gifts. These gifts, described in passages such as 1 Corinthians 12, Romans 12, and Ephesians 4, are given to believers for the purpose of building up the Church and carrying out its mission.

These gifts include a wide range of abilities, such as teaching, healing, prophecy, and leadership. Each believer is given at least one spiritual gift, which they are called to use in service to others. The variety of gifts ensures that the Church is equipped to meet the diverse needs of its members and to effectively carry out the work of the kingdom.

12.4.3 Empowerment for Spiritual Growth

The Holy Spirit also empowers believers for spiritual growth. The Spirit works within believers to produce the fruit of the Spirit—love, joy, peace, patience, kindness, goodness, faithfulness, gentleness, and self-control (Galatians 5:22-23). These qualities reflect the character of Jesus and are evidence of the Spirit's transformative work in the lives of believers.

This empowerment for spiritual growth is a continuation of Jesus' prophetic work, as it enables believers to live out the teachings of Jesus in their daily lives. The Holy Spirit helps believers to overcome sin, to grow in holiness, and to become more like Christ.

12.5 The Comforting Work of the Holy Spirit

Another important aspect of the Holy Spirit's work is to comfort and encourage believers. Jesus referred to the Holy

Spirit as the Comforter, indicating that the Spirit would provide the support and reassurance needed for believers to endure the challenges of life and faith.

12.5.1 The Presence of the Spirit

The presence of the Holy Spirit is a source of comfort for believers, as it assures them that they are not alone. The Spirit's indwelling presence is a continual reminder of God's love and faithfulness, providing peace and assurance even in difficult circumstances.

The Holy Spirit also brings comfort by interceding for believers in prayer. In Romans 8:26-27, Paul writes, "Likewise the Spirit also helps in our weaknesses. For we do not know what we should pray for as we ought, but the Spirit Himself makes intercession for us with groanings which cannot be uttered. Now He who searches the hearts knows what the mind of the Spirit is, because He makes intercession for the saints according to the will of God."

This intercession is a profound source of comfort, as it assures believers that their needs and concerns are being brought before God, even when they are unable to articulate them.

12.5.2 Encouragement in Trials

The Holy Spirit also provides encouragement in times of trial and suffering. Jesus warned His disciples that they would face persecution and hardship, but He promised that the Holy Spirit would be with them, giving them the strength and courage to persevere.

Throughout the New Testament, we see the Holy Spirit comforting and encouraging believers in the midst of trials. For example, in Acts 4, when Peter and John were threatened by the authorities, they prayed for boldness, and the Holy Spirit filled them, enabling them to continue preaching with courage.

The comforting work of the Holy Spirit is a continuation of Jesus' own ministry of encouragement and support. Just as Jesus comforted His disciples with His presence and words, so the Holy Spirit continues to comfort believers today.

12.6 The Holy Spirit and the Mission of the Church

The Holy Spirit's work in continuing Jesus' prophetic ministry is closely tied to the mission of the Church. Jesus commissioned His disciples to go into all the world and make disciples of all nations (Matthew 28:19-20). This Great Commission is carried out through the power and guidance of the Holy Spirit.

12.6.1 The Holy Spirit as the Missionary Spirit

The Holy Spirit is often referred to as the "missionary Spirit" because of the Spirit's role in guiding and empowering the Church's mission

. From the day of Pentecost onward, the Holy Spirit has been the driving force behind the spread of the Gospel.

The book of Acts is filled with examples of the Holy Spirit leading the apostles and other believers in their missionary efforts. The Spirit directed Philip to the Ethiopian eunuch, guided Peter to the house of Cornelius, and called Paul and Barnabas to their missionary journeys. In each case, the Holy Spirit was actively involved in advancing the mission of the Church.

12.6.2 The Global Expansion of the Church

The Holy Spirit's work has not been limited to the early Church but continues to drive the global expansion of the Church today. The Spirit is at work in every part of the world, raising up believers, empowering missionaries, and bringing people to faith in Christ.

The global expansion of the Church is a testament to the ongoing work of the Holy Spirit in continuing Jesus' prophetic ministry. The Church's growth and influence are not the result of human effort alone but are the fruit of the Spirit's work in the hearts and lives of people around the world.

12.6.3 The Unity of the Church

The Holy Spirit also plays a crucial role in maintaining the unity of the Church. In John 17, Jesus prayed for the unity of His followers, that they would be one just as He and the Father are one (John 17:21). This unity is made possible by the Holy Spirit, who binds believers together in love and fellowship.

The Holy Spirit works to overcome divisions and conflicts within the Church, fostering a spirit of reconciliation and mutual support. This unity is essential for the Church's witness to the world, as Jesus said that the world would know His disciples by their love for one another (John 13:35).

12.7 The Holy Spirit and the Future Fulfillment of Jesus' Work

While the Holy Spirit continues Jesus' prophetic work on Earth, this work is also oriented toward the future. The Holy Spirit not only reminds believers of what Jesus has done but also points them forward to the future fulfillment of God's promises.

12.7.1 The Spirit as the Guarantee of Future Inheritance

The Holy Spirit is described in the New Testament as the "guarantee" or "down payment" of the believer's future inheritance (Ephesians 1:13-14). This means that the presence of the Holy Spirit in the life of a believer is a foretaste of the glory that is to come. The Spirit's work in the present is a sign that God will fulfill His promises and that believers will one day share in the fullness of the kingdom of God.

This future orientation of the Holy Spirit's work gives believers hope and confidence as they live out their faith in the present. The Spirit assures them that, despite the challenges and struggles they may face, God's plan is moving forward, and they are part of that plan.

12.7.2 The Spirit's Role in the Return of Christ

The Holy Spirit also plays a role in preparing the Church for the return of Christ. The Spirit works to purify and sanctify believers, making them ready for the day when Jesus will return to establish His kingdom in its fullness.

In Revelation 22:17, the Spirit and the bride (the Church) together say, "Come!" This longing for the return of Christ is inspired by the Holy Spirit, who keeps the Church focused on the hope of Christ's return and the final consummation of God's plan.

12.8 Conclusion

The Holy Spirit's role as the continuation of Jesus' prophetic work is central to the life and mission of the Church. Through teaching, guiding, empowering, and comforting believers, the Holy Spirit ensures that Jesus' work on Earth continues and that the Church remains faithful to its calling.

The Holy Spirit's work is not limited to maintaining what Jesus began but also involves leading the Church into new understandings and applications of the Gospel, empowering believers for witness and service, and preparing the Church for the future fulfillment of God's promises.

As believers, we are called to be attentive to the work of the Holy Spirit in our lives and in the life of the Church. By listening to the Spirit's guidance, relying on the Spirit's power, and embracing the Spirit's comfort, we participate in the ongoing mission of Jesus and contribute to the advancement of God's kingdom on Earth. The Holy Spirit is not just a continuation of Jesus' work; the Spirit is the active presence of Jesus with us, ensuring that His prophetic ministry continues to bear fruit until the day He returns in glory.

CHAPTER 05

THE HOLY SPIRIT AND THE DEITY OF CHRIST

Witnessing to Jesus' Divine Nature: The Holy Spirit's Testimony About Jesus

13.1 Introduction

The Holy Spirit plays a vital role in revealing and affirming the divine nature of Jesus Christ. Throughout the New Testament, the Holy Spirit bears witness to Jesus' identity as the Son of God, both through the testimony of Scripture and through the transformative work in the lives of believers. Understanding the Holy Spirit's testimony about Jesus is crucial for grasping the full scope of Christian theology and for deepening our faith in Christ's divine nature. In this chapter, we will explore how the Holy Spirit witnesses to the deity of Christ, the various ways this testimony is manifested, and the implications of this witness for the Church and individual believers.

13.2 The Holy Spirit as the Spirit of Truth

In the Gospel of John, Jesus refers to the Holy Spirit as the "Spirit of truth" (John 14:17; 16:13). This title highlights the Holy Spirit's role in revealing the truth about God, and particularly the truth about Jesus. The Spirit of truth is the one who leads believers into a deeper understanding of who Jesus is, ensuring that the Church remains anchored in the correct doctrine of Christ's divinity.

13.2.1 The Spirit's Role in Revealing Jesus' Identity

One of the primary functions of the Holy Spirit is to reveal Jesus' true identity as the Son of God. During Jesus' earthly ministry, the Holy Spirit was active in affirming His divine nature. For example, at Jesus' baptism, the Holy Spirit descended upon Him like a dove, and a voice from heaven declared, "This is My beloved Son, in whom I am well pleased" (Matthew 3:16-17). This event served as a public affirmation of Jesus' divine sonship, witnessed by those present.

Throughout the Gospels, the Holy Spirit continues to reveal Jesus' identity through His miracles, teachings, and fulfillment of Old Testament prophecies. The Spirit's work is to point people to Jesus, helping them to recognize that He is not just a prophet or teacher, but God incarnate.

13.2.2 The Spirit's Witness in the Early Church

After Jesus' ascension, the Holy Spirit continued to bear witness to Jesus' divine nature in the early Church. The apostles, filled with the Holy Spirit at Pentecost, boldly proclaimed Jesus as the risen Lord and the Son of God. In Acts 2:32-36, Peter, empowered by the Holy Spirit, declared, "This Jesus God has raised up, of which we are all witnesses... Therefore let all the house of Israel know assuredly that God has made this Jesus, whom you crucified, both Lord and Christ."

The Holy Spirit's testimony through the apostles was crucial in establishing the early Church's understanding of Jesus' divinity. The Spirit's witness provided the foundation for the Church's confession that Jesus is "Lord," a title that affirms His divine status and authority.

13.3 The Testimony of Scripture and the Holy Spirit

The Holy Spirit is intimately involved in the inspiration of Scripture, which serves as the written testimony to Jesus' divine nature. The Scriptures, both Old and New Testaments, bear witness to the identity of Jesus as the Son of God, and the Holy Spirit plays a key role in guiding believers to understand and accept this testimony.

13.3.1 The Inspiration of Scripture

The apostle Paul writes in 2 Timothy 3:16, "All Scripture is given by inspiration of God," and in 2 Peter 1:21, Peter states, "For prophecy never came by the will of man, but holy men of God spoke as they were moved by the Holy Spirit." These verses emphasize the role of the Holy Spirit in the writing of Scripture, ensuring that the biblical authors accurately recorded God's revelation, including the revelation of Jesus' divine nature.

The Old Testament contains numerous prophecies and types that point to the coming of the Messiah, many of which find their fulfillment in Jesus. The Holy Spirit inspired these writings, preparing the way for the full revelation of Jesus in the New Testament. For example, the prophecy of Isaiah 9:6, which speaks of a child who will be called "Wonderful Counselor, Mighty God, Everlasting Father, Prince of Peace," finds its fulfillment in Jesus Christ.

13.3.2 The Illumination of Scripture

In addition to inspiring Scripture, the Holy Spirit also illuminates the minds of believers, helping them to understand and apply the truths of Scripture, particularly those concerning Jesus' divine nature. The Spirit opens the eyes of believers to see the glory of Christ in the pages of the Bible.

In 1 Corinthians 2:10-14, Paul explains that the deep things of God are revealed by the Spirit, who enables believers to discern spiritual truths. Without the Holy Spirit, the true significance of Jesus' identity and work would remain hidden. The Spirit's illumination ensures that believers can recognize Jesus as the Son of God and respond to Him in faith.

13.4 The Holy Spirit's Testimony in the Life of Jesus

The life and ministry of Jesus were marked by the active presence of the Holy Spirit, who continually testified to His divine nature. From His conception to His resurrection, the Holy Spirit was involved in every aspect of Jesus' life, bearing witness to His identity as the Son of God.

13.4.1 The Conception of Jesus

The miraculous conception of Jesus is one of the earliest and most profound testimonies to His divine nature. According to Luke 1:35, the angel Gabriel announced to Mary that the Holy Spirit would come upon her, and the power of the Most High would overshadow her, resulting in the birth of a holy child, the Son of God.

This divine conception, brought about by the Holy Spirit, set Jesus apart from all other human beings. It affirmed that He was not merely a man but the incarnate Word of God, fully divine and fully human.

13.4.2 The Baptism of Jesus

As mentioned earlier, the baptism of Jesus is another significant moment where the Holy Spirit testified to His divine nature. The descent of the Holy Spirit in the form of a dove and the voice from heaven declaring Jesus as God's beloved Son served as a public endorsement of His identity and mission.

This event also marked the beginning of Jesus' public ministry, during which the Holy Spirit empowered Him to perform miracles, preach the Gospel, and fulfill His redemptive work. The presence and activity of the Holy Spirit throughout Jesus' ministry continually pointed to His divine origin and authority.

13.4.3 The Resurrection of Jesus

The resurrection of Jesus is the ultimate testimony to His divine nature, and the Holy Spirit played a crucial role in this event. In Romans 1:4, Paul writes that Jesus was "declared to be the Son of God with power according to the Spirit of holiness, by the resurrection from the dead." The Holy Spirit's involvement in raising Jesus from the dead serves as the definitive proof of His divinity.

The resurrection vindicated Jesus' claims to be the Son of God and confirmed that He had conquered sin and death. The Holy Spirit's role in the resurrection is a powerful witness to Jesus' divine nature and His authority as the Lord of all.

13.5 The Holy Spirit's Witness in the Life of Believers

The testimony of the Holy Spirit to Jesus' divine nature is not limited to historical events; it is also evident in the ongoing work of the Spirit in the lives of believers. The Holy Spirit continues to bear witness to Jesus' identity through the transformation of lives, the experience of God's presence, and the empowerment for mission.

13.5.1 The Spirit's Work in Regeneration

One of the primary ways the Holy Spirit testifies to Jesus' divine nature is through the work of regeneration. When a person comes to faith in Christ, the Holy Spirit brings about a new birth, transforming the believer's heart and mind. This new birth is a powerful testimony to the divine nature of Jesus, as it is through faith in Him that this transformation occurs.

In John 3:5-6, Jesus speaks to Nicodemus about the necessity of being "born of the Spirit" in order to enter the kingdom of God. This new birth, brought about by the Holy Spirit, is a witness to the divine power and authority of Jesus, who alone can grant eternal life.

13.5.2 The Spirit's Assurance of Sonship

The Holy Spirit also bears witness to Jesus' divine nature by assuring believers of their adoption as children of God. In Romans 8:15-16, Paul writes, "For you did not receive the spirit of bondage again to fear, but you received the Spirit of adoption by whom we cry out, 'Abba, Father.' The Spirit Himself bears witness with our spirit that we are children of God."

This assurance of sonship is rooted in the believer's relationship with Jesus Christ, the Son of God. The Holy Spirit's testimony within the believer affirms that through Jesus, they have been brought into the family of God and can relate to God as their Father.

13.5.3 The Spirit's Empowerment for Witness

The Holy Spirit continues to testify to Jesus' divine nature by empowering believers to bear witness to Him. In Acts 1:8, Jesus promised His disciples that they would receive power when the Holy Spirit came upon them, enabling them to be His witnesses "in Jerusalem, and in all Judea and Samaria, and to the end of the earth."

The boldness and effectiveness of the apostles' witness, as recorded in the book of Acts, is a direct result of the Holy Spirit's empowerment. The Spirit's work in spreading the Gospel and confirming the truth of Jesus' divinity through signs and wonders is a powerful testimony to who Jesus is.

This empowerment continues in the life of the Church today, as the Holy Spirit enables believers to proclaim the Gospel and to demonstrate the reality of Jesus' divine nature through their words and actions.

13.6 The Implications of the Holy Spirit's Testimony

The Holy Spirit's testimony to the divine nature of Jesus has profound implications for both the Church and individual believers. Understanding and responding to this testimony is essential for a vibrant and authentic Christian faith.

13.6.1 Affirming the Deity of Christ

The Holy Spirit's witness affirms the central Christian doctrine of the deity of Christ. This affirmation is foundational to the Christian faith, as it distinguishes Jesus from all other religious leaders and teachers. Recognizing Jesus as fully God and fully man is crucial for understanding the significance of His life, death, and resurrection.

The Church, therefore, is called to uphold and proclaim the doctrine of Christ's deity, resisting any attempts to diminish or distort this truth. The Holy Spirit's testimony serves as a safeguard against false teachings and ensures that the Church remains faithful to the Gospel.

13.6.2 Cultivating a Christ-Centered Faith

The Holy Spirit's witness to Jesus' divine nature calls believers to cultivate a Christ-centered faith. Since the Holy Spirit's primary role is to glorify Jesus and to reveal His identity, believers are encouraged to focus their faith and devotion on Christ. This involves deepening their understanding of who Jesus is, growing in their relationship with Him, and allowing His presence to shape every aspect of their lives.

A Christ-centered faith is also characterized by a reliance on the Holy Spirit, who enables believers to live out the teachings of Jesus and to reflect His character in their daily lives.

13.6.3 Empowerment for Mission

The Holy Spirit's testimony to the deity of Christ also has implications for the Church's mission. As the Holy Spirit empowers believers to bear witness to Jesus, they are called to share the truth of His divine nature with others. This mission involves both proclamation and demonstration—proclaiming the Gospel and demonstrating the reality of Jesus' lordship through lives transformed by the Spirit.

The Church's mission is not carried out in human strength but in the power of the Holy Spirit, who continues to testify to Jesus' divine nature through the Church's witness.

13.7 Conclusion

The Holy Spirit's testimony to the divine nature of Jesus is a central theme in the New Testament and a foundational aspect of the Christian faith. Through the inspiration and illumination of Scripture, the testimony in the life and ministry of Jesus, and the ongoing work in the lives of believers, the Holy Spirit continually bears witness to the truth that Jesus is the Son of God, fully divine and fully human.

This testimony is essential for understanding who Jesus is and for responding to Him in faith. It calls believers to affirm the deity of Christ, to cultivate a Christ-centered faith, and to engage in the mission of proclaiming and demonstrating the reality of Jesus' divine nature to the world.

As we reflect on the Holy Spirit's testimony, we are reminded that our faith is not based on human wisdom or tradition but on the revelation of God through His Spirit. The Holy Spirit, as the Spirit of truth, continues to lead us into a deeper understanding of Jesus and to empower us to live out the truth of His divine nature in our lives and in the life of the Church.

Revealing Jesus' Authority: How the Holy Spirit Highlights Jesus' Authority Over Creation, Sin, and Death

14.1 Introduction

The authority of Jesus Christ is a central theme in the New Testament, encompassing His dominion over all creation, His power to forgive sins, and His victory over death. The Holy Spirit plays a crucial role in revealing and affirming this authority, both during Jesus' earthly ministry and in the ongoing life of the Church. In this chapter, we will explore how the Holy Spirit highlights Jesus' authority over creation, sin, and death, and the implications of this authority for believers.

14.2 Jesus' Authority Over Creation

One of the most significant aspects of Jesus' authority is His dominion over creation. The New Testament presents Jesus as the agent of creation, the one through whom all things were made, and as the sustainer of the universe. The Holy Spirit reveals and affirms this authority in several key ways.

14.2.1 The Role of the Holy Spirit in Creation

The Bible teaches that the Holy Spirit was involved in the creation of the world. In Genesis 1:2, the Spirit of God is described as hovering over the waters, bringing order out of chaos. This creative activity is later echoed in the New Testament, where Jesus is identified as the divine Word through whom all things were made (John 1:1-3).

The connection between the Holy Spirit and Jesus in creation highlights Jesus' authority over the natural world. The Holy Spirit, who was present at creation, testifies to Jesus' role as the Creator and sustainer of all things. This testimony is evident in the miracles that Jesus performed, which demonstrated His power over nature.

14.2.2 Miracles as Testimonies to Jesus' Authority

Throughout His ministry, Jesus performed numerous miracles that revealed His authority over creation. These miracles, such as calming the storm (Mark 4:35-41), walking on water (Matthew 14:22-33), and multiplying the loaves and fishes (John 6:1-14), were not merely acts of compassion but were also signs that pointed to His divine authority.

The Holy Spirit played a crucial role in these miracles, empowering Jesus to exercise His authority over the natural world. In the Gospel of John, these miraculous signs are presented as evidence that Jesus is the Son of God, with power over all creation. The Spirit's work in these miracles testifies to the reality of Jesus' authority and invites believers to recognize and trust in His power.

14.2.3 The Holy Spirit in the Life of Believers

The Holy Spirit continues to reveal Jesus' authority over creation in the lives of believers. This is evident in the Spirit's work in answering prayers, providing for needs, and performing miracles in the lives of Christians today. These acts of divine intervention serve as reminders that Jesus is still sovereign over all creation and that His authority extends to every aspect of the natural world.

For believers, this understanding of Jesus' authority over creation brings comfort and assurance, knowing that the same power that created and sustains the universe is at work in their lives. It also calls for a response of worship and obedience, recognizing Jesus as the Lord of all.

14.3 Jesus' Authority Over Sin

Another key aspect of Jesus' authority is His power to forgive sins. Throughout His ministry, Jesus repeatedly demonstrated His authority to forgive sins, a power that belongs to God alone. The Holy Spirit plays a vital role in revealing this authority and in bringing people to a place of repentance and forgiveness.

14.3.1 The Forgiveness of Sins in Jesus' Ministry

One of the most striking examples of Jesus' authority to forgive sins is found in the story of the paralytic in Mark 2:1-12. When the paralytic was brought to Jesus, He said to him, "Son, your sins are forgiven." This declaration shocked the religious leaders present, who questioned Jesus' authority to forgive sins. In response, Jesus healed the man, saying, "But that you may know that the Son of Man has power on earth to forgive sins" (Mark 2:10).

This miracle, like many others, was performed in the power of the Holy Spirit. The Spirit's presence in Jesus' ministry was a continual witness to His authority over sin. The healing of the paralytic not only demonstrated Jesus' compassion but also revealed His divine prerogative to forgive sins, affirming His identity as the Son of God.

14.3.2 The Holy Spirit's Role in Conviction and Repentance

The Holy Spirit also plays a crucial role in convicting people of their sins and leading them to repentance. In John 16:8, Jesus said that the Holy Spirit would "convict the world of sin, and of righteousness, and of judgment." This conviction is the first step in recognizing Jesus' authority over sin, as it brings individuals to an awareness of their need for forgiveness.

Through the work of the Holy Spirit, people are drawn to Jesus, who alone has the authority to forgive sins. The Spirit opens their hearts to the reality of their sinfulness and the sufficiency of Jesus' atoning sacrifice. This process of conviction and repentance is a powerful testimony to Jesus' authority over sin and His ability to bring about transformation in the lives of those who turn to Him in faith.

14.3.3 Justification and Sanctification by the Spirit

The Holy Spirit also plays a key role in the believer's experience of justification and sanctification, both of which are rooted in Jesus' authority over sin. Justification is the act of being declared righteous before God, and it is made possible through faith in Jesus' atoning death and resurrection. The Holy Spirit applies the work of Christ to the believer, bringing them into a right relationship with God.

Sanctification, the process of becoming more like Christ, is also the work of the Holy Spirit. The Spirit empowers believers to overcome sin and to live lives that reflect the holiness and righteousness of Jesus. This ongoing work of the Spirit in the life of the believer is a continual testimony to Jesus' authority over sin and His power to bring about true and lasting change.

14.4 Jesus' Authority Over Death

The ultimate expression of Jesus' authority is His victory over death. Through His death and resurrection, Jesus conquered the power of death, offering eternal life to all who believe in Him. The Holy Spirit is instrumental in revealing and affirming this authority, both in the resurrection of Jesus and in the hope of resurrection for all believers.

14.4.1 The Resurrection of Jesus

The resurrection of Jesus is the cornerstone of Christian faith and the ultimate demonstration of His authority over death. The New Testament repeatedly affirms that the Holy Spirit played a central role in raising Jesus from the dead. In Romans 8:11, Paul writes, "But if the Spirit of Him who raised Jesus from the dead dwells in you, He who raised Christ from the dead will also give life to your mortal bodies through His Spirit who dwells in you."

The Holy Spirit's involvement in the resurrection is a powerful testimony to Jesus' divine authority. By raising Jesus from the dead, the Spirit confirmed that Jesus is the Son of God, who has triumphed over sin and death. The resurrection is the ultimate proof that Jesus has the power to give life and that His promises of eternal life are trustworthy.

14.4.2 The Promise of Resurrection for Believers

The Holy Spirit also plays a crucial role in the believer's hope of resurrection. The same Spirit who raised Jesus from the dead dwells in believers, guaranteeing that they, too, will share in the resurrection. This promise is a central aspect of the Christian hope, as it assures believers that death is not the end and that they will be raised to eternal life with Christ.

In Ephesians 1:13-14, Paul speaks of the Holy Spirit as the "guarantee of our inheritance until the redemption of the purchased possession." This guarantee is a testimony to Jesus' authority over death and a source of assurance for believers as they look forward to the fulfillment of God's promises.

14.4.3 Victory Over Death in the Life of the Church

The Holy Spirit continues to reveal Jesus' authority over death in the life of the Church. This is evident in the way believers face death with hope and confidence, knowing that Jesus has conquered the grave. The Spirit's presence in the lives of believers provides comfort and assurance, especially in times of suffering and loss.

The Church's proclamation of the resurrection is also a powerful testimony to Jesus' authority. Through the preaching of the Gospel and the celebration of the sacraments, the Church bears witness to the reality of Jesus' victory over death and the hope of eternal life. The Holy Spirit empowers the Church to continue this witness, ensuring that the message of Jesus' authority is proclaimed to all the world.

14.5 The Implications of Jesus' Authority

The Holy Spirit's revelation of Jesus' authority over creation, sin, and death has profound implications for believers and the Church. Understanding and responding to this authority is essential for living a life of faith and obedience.

14.5.1 Submission to Jesus' Lordship

The revelation of Jesus' authority calls for a response of submission to His lordship. As the one who has authority over all creation, sin, and death, Jesus is worthy of our worship, obedience, and trust. The Holy Spirit works in the hearts of believers to bring them into alignment with Jesus' will, guiding them to live lives that reflect His authority and lordship.

Submission to Jesus' authority also involves recognizing His sovereignty in every area of life. This means trusting Him in times of uncertainty, relying on His power to overcome sin, and holding fast to the hope of resurrection. The Holy Spirit helps believers to grow in their understanding of what it means to live under the lordship of Christ, empowering them to walk in obedience and faith.

14.5.2 Proclamation of the Gospel

The Holy Spirit's revelation of Jesus' authority also fuels the Church's mission to proclaim the Gospel. The message of Jesus' authority over creation, sin, and death is at the heart of the Gospel, and it is the foundation of the Church's witness to the world. The Holy Spirit empowers believers to share this message with boldness and conviction, calling others to recognize and submit to Jesus' authority.

The proclamation of the Gospel is not just about words but also about demonstrating the reality of Jesus' authority in the lives of believers. Through acts of compassion, justice, and love, the Church bears witness to the transformative power of Jesus' authority, showing the world what it means to live under His lordship.

14.5.3 Hope in the Face of Suffering and Death

Finally, the revelation of Jesus' authority over death provides believers with hope in the face of suffering and death. The Holy Spirit comforts and strengthens believers, reminding them of the promises of resurrection and eternal life. This hope enables believers to face suffering with courage and to endure trials with perseverance, knowing that Jesus has overcome the world.

The Holy Spirit's witness to Jesus' authority over death also shapes the way believers approach death. Rather than fearing death, believers can face it with confidence, knowing that it is not the end but the gateway to eternal life with Christ. This hope is a powerful testimony to the world, pointing to the reality of Jesus' victory over death and the promise of life everlasting.

14.6 Conclusion

The Holy Spirit plays a crucial role in revealing and affirming Jesus' authority over creation, sin, and death. Through the testimony of Scripture, the empowerment of Jesus' ministry, and the ongoing work in the lives of believers, the Holy Spirit highlights the reality of Jesus' divine authority and invites believers to respond in faith and obedience.

Understanding Jesus' authority is essential for a vibrant and faithful Christian life. It calls for submission to His lordship, fuels the Church's mission to proclaim the Gospel, and provides hope in the face of suffering and death. The Holy Spirit's revelation of this authority is a continual source of strength and assurance for believers, guiding them to live lives that reflect the power and glory of Jesus Christ.

As we reflect on the Holy Spirit's work in revealing Jesus' authority, we are reminded of the profound truth that Jesus is Lord over all creation, the one who has conquered sin and death, and the one who holds the keys to eternal life. This truth is the foundation of our faith and the source of our hope, as we look forward to the day when Jesus' authority will be fully revealed and His kingdom established in all its fullness.

The Unity of the Trinity: Understanding the Relationship Between the Father, Son, and Holy Spirit

15.1 Introduction

The doctrine of the Trinity is one of the most profound and mysterious aspects of Christian theology. It asserts that there is one God who exists in three distinct persons: the Father, the Son, and the Holy Spirit. These three persons are co-equal, co-eternal, and of one essence, yet they are distinct in their relationships and roles within the Godhead. Understanding the unity of the Trinity is essential for grasping the nature of God as revealed in Scripture and for deepening our relationship with Him. In this chapter, we will explore the biblical foundation for the doctrine of the Trinity, examine the relationship between the Father, Son, and Holy Spirit, and consider the implications of this unity for the Christian faith.

15.2 The Biblical Foundation for the Trinity

The word "Trinity" does not appear in the Bible, but the concept is clearly present throughout both the Old and New Testaments. The doctrine of the Trinity is derived from the full witness of Scripture, which consistently reveals one God who exists in three persons.

15.2.1 The Oneness of God

The Bible is emphatic in its teaching that there is only one God. This monotheistic belief is foundational to the Jewish and Christian faiths. In Deuteronomy 6:4, known as the Shema, we read, "Hear, O Israel: The Lord our God, the Lord is one!" This verse affirms the oneness of God, a truth that is echoed throughout the Old Testament.

Isaiah 45:5 further emphasizes this point: "I am the Lord, and there is no other; apart from me there is no God." The oneness of God is a central tenet of biblical faith, and any understanding of the Trinity must begin with this foundational truth.

15.2.2 The Plurality Within the Godhead

While the Bible teaches that there is one God, it also reveals a plurality within the Godhead. This is evident from the very beginning of Scripture. In Genesis 1:26, God says, "Let Us make man in Our image, according to Our likeness." The use of the plural pronouns "Us" and "Our" suggests a complexity within the unity of God.

The plurality within the Godhead is further hinted at in passages such as Genesis 11:7, where God says, "Come, let Us go down and confuse their language," and Isaiah 6:8, where God asks, "Whom shall I send, and who will go for Us?" These passages do not explicitly define the Trinity, but they point to the reality that God exists in more than one person.

15.2.3 The Revelation of the Trinity in the New Testament

The New Testament provides a clearer revelation of the Trinity, particularly in the relationship between the Father, Son, and Holy Spirit. The baptism of Jesus is one of the most significant Trinitarian passages in the Bible. In Matthew 3:16-17, we read, "When He had been baptized, Jesus came up immediately from the water; and behold, the heavens were opened to Him, and He saw the Spirit of God descending like a dove and alighting upon Him. And suddenly a voice came from heaven, saying, 'This is My beloved Son, in whom I am well pleased.'"

In this passage, all three persons of the Trinity are present and active: the Father speaks from heaven, the Son is baptized, and the Holy Spirit descends upon the Son in the form of a dove. This event vividly portrays the distinct roles and unity of the Father, Son, and Holy Spirit.

Another key passage is the Great Commission in Matthew 28:19, where Jesus instructs His disciples to baptize "in the name of the Father and of the Son and of the Holy Spirit." The singular "name" (not "names") used in conjunction with the three persons highlights the unity and equality of the Trinity.

The apostle Paul also reflects a Trinitarian understanding in his writings. In 2 Corinthians 13:14, he writes, "The grace of the Lord Jesus Christ, and the love of God, and the communion of the Holy Spirit be with you all." This benediction recognizes the distinct roles of each person of the Trinity while affirming their unity in blessing the believers.

15.3 The Distinct Roles Within the Trinity

While the Father, Son, and Holy Spirit are united in essence, they have distinct roles within the Godhead. These roles are not hierarchical in terms of value or divinity but reflect the way in which the three persons relate to one another and to creation.

15.3.1 The Role of the Father

In Scripture, the Father is often depicted as the source or originator within the Trinity. He is the one who initiates creation, salvation, and the plan of redemption. The Father is described as the one who sent the Son into the world to accomplish the work of salvation (John 3:16-17). He is also the one to whom Jesus prays and submits His will (Matthew 26:39).

The Father's role as the source is seen in passages like Ephesians 1:3-6, where Paul praises the Father for blessing believers with every spiritual blessing in Christ and for predestining them for adoption as sons through Jesus Christ. The Father's love and initiative in the work of salvation are central to His role within the Trinity.

15.3.2 The Role of the Son

The Son, Jesus Christ, is the Word of God made flesh (John 1:14). He is the agent of creation (John 1:3; Colossians 1:16) and the one who accomplishes the work of redemption through His incarnation, life, death, and resurrection. The Son reveals the Father to humanity (John 14:9) and is the mediator between God and humanity (1 Timothy 2:5).

Jesus willingly submits to the Father's will, as seen in the Garden of Gethsemane (Matthew 26:39), but this submission does not imply inferiority. Rather, it reflects the unity and harmony within the Trinity, where each person willingly fulfills their role in the divine plan.

The Son's role is also central to the concept of eternal life. In John 17:3, Jesus prays, "And this is eternal life, that they may know You, the only true God, and Jesus Christ whom You have sent." Knowing the Son is essential for knowing the Father, and through the Son, believers are brought into a relationship with the triune God.

15.3.3 The Role of the Holy Spirit

The Holy Spirit is often described as the executor of the Father and Son's will. He is the one who applies the work of redemption to believers, regenerating them, indwelling them, and empowering them for godly living. The Spirit is also the one who sanctifies believers, leading them into all truth and helping them to grow in Christlikeness (John 16:13; Romans 8:9-11).

The Holy Spirit's role as the one who reveals and glorifies Christ is emphasized in John 16:14, where Jesus says, "He will glorify Me, for He will take of what is Mine and declare it to you." The Spirit does not act independently of the Father and Son but works in perfect unity with them to accomplish the divine purposes.

The Holy Spirit's indwelling presence in the life of believers is a profound expression of the Trinity's unity. Through the Spirit, believers are brought into fellowship with the Father and the Son, experiencing the fullness of God's presence in their lives (John 14:16-17; Romans 8:14-16).

15.4 The Unity of the Trinity in Salvation

The unity of the Trinity is most vividly displayed in the work of salvation. The Father, Son, and Holy Spirit each play distinct roles, yet they work together in perfect harmony to bring about the redemption of humanity.

15.4.1 The Father's Role in Salvation

The Father is the architect of salvation, having planned it from eternity past. Ephesians 1:4-5 says, "He chose us in Him before the foundation of the world, that we should be holy and without blame before Him in love, having predestined us to adoption as sons by Jesus Christ to Himself, according to the good pleasure of His will." The Father's role in salvation involves choosing, predestining, and sending the Son to accomplish redemption.

The Father's love is the motivation behind the plan of salvation. John 3:16 famously declares, "For God so loved the world that He gave His only begotten Son, that whoever believes in Him should not perish but have everlasting life." The Father's love for the world is demonstrated in His willingness to give His Son as a sacrifice for sin.

15.4.2 The Son's Role in Salvation

The Son's role in salvation is to accomplish the work of redemption through His incarnation, life, death, and resurrection. Jesus took on human flesh (John 1:14), lived a sinless life (Hebrews 4:15), and offered Himself as a perfect sacrifice for the sins of the world (1 John 2:2). Through His death on the cross, Jesus satisfied the demands of God's justice and made a way for humanity to be reconciled to God (2 Corinthians 5:21).

The resurrection of Jesus is the Father's vindication of the Son's work, demonstrating that Jesus' sacrifice was sufficient and that death has been defeated (Romans 4:25). The Son's ascension to the right hand of the Father and His ongoing intercession for believers (Hebrews 7:25) are also central to

His role in the work of salvation.

15.4.3 The Holy Spirit's Role in Salvation

The Holy Spirit's role in salvation is to apply the work of Christ to the lives of believers. The Spirit regenerates those who believe, bringing them from spiritual death to life (John 3:5-6; Titus 3:5). The Spirit also indwells believers, sealing them for the day of redemption and guaranteeing their inheritance (Ephesians 1:13-14).

The Holy Spirit sanctifies believers, transforming them into the image of Christ and empowering them to live holy lives (2 Corinthians 3:18; Galatians 5:22-23). The Spirit's work in the life of believers is a testimony to the unity of the Trinity, as the Spirit brings the presence of the Father and the Son into the believer's life (John 14:16-17).

The unity of the Trinity in salvation is a profound demonstration of the triune God's love, grace, and power. Each person of the Trinity works in perfect harmony to accomplish the redemption of humanity, revealing the depth of God's commitment to bringing people into a relationship with Himself.

15.5 Theological and Practical Implications of the Trinity

The doctrine of the Trinity is not merely an abstract theological concept; it has significant implications for Christian faith and practice. Understanding the unity of the Trinity shapes our worship, our understanding of God's nature, and our relationships with one another.

15.5.1 Worship of the Triune God

The unity of the Trinity calls believers to worship God in His fullness. Worshiping the triune God means recognizing and honoring the Father, Son, and Holy Spirit as co-equal and co-eternal persons. Christian worship is Trinitarian at its core, as it is directed to the Father, through the Son, and in the power of the Holy Spirit.

The unity of the Trinity also guards against the worship of a fragmented or incomplete understanding of God. It reminds believers that God is one in essence and three in persons, and that true worship involves acknowledging and adoring the fullness of God's nature as revealed in Scripture.

15.5.2 Understanding God's Nature and Love

The doctrine of the Trinity provides insight into the nature of God's love. The relationship between the Father,

Son, and Holy Spirit is characterized by perfect love, unity, and mutual glorification. This intra-Trinitarian love is the source and model for the love that God extends to humanity.

In John 17:24-26, Jesus prays, "Father, I desire that they also whom You gave Me may be with Me where I am, that they may behold My glory which You have given Me; for You loved Me before the foundation of the world... that the love with which You loved Me may be in them, and I in them." The love shared within the Trinity is the basis for the love that believers experience in their relationship with God.

Understanding the Trinity also deepens our comprehension of God's nature as both transcendent and immanent. God is transcendent, existing beyond and independent of creation, yet He is also immanent, personally involved in the world through the incarnation of the Son and the indwelling presence of the Holy Spirit.

15.5.3 Reflecting Trinitarian Unity in Relationships

The unity of the Trinity serves as a model for Christian relationships, particularly within the Church. Just as the Father, Son, and Holy Spirit are united in love and purpose, so too are believers called to live in unity with one another. In John 17:21, Jesus prays that His followers "may be one, as You, Father, are in Me, and I in You; that they also may be one in Us."

This call to unity is rooted in the Trinitarian nature of God. The Church, as the body of Christ, is to reflect the unity of the Trinity in its relationships, striving for harmony, mutual love, and cooperation in the work of the Gospel. The Holy Spirit plays a crucial role in fostering this unity, as He indwells believers and binds them together in the bond of peace (Ephesians 4:3).

The unity of the Trinity also has implications for other relationships, such as marriage and family. In Ephesians 5:31-32, Paul compares the relationship between husband and wife to the relationship between Christ and the Church, which is rooted in the love and unity of the Trinity. Christian marriages and families are called to reflect the self-giving love and unity that characterizes the relationship within the Trinity.

15.6 Conclusion

The doctrine of the Trinity is a profound and essential aspect of Christian theology, revealing the nature of God as one in essence and three in persons: the Father, the Son, and the Holy Spirit. The unity of the Trinity is not merely a theological concept but a reality that has significant implications for our understanding of God, our worship, and our relationships with one another.

Throughout Scripture, the Father, Son, and Holy Spirit are shown to be united in their essence, purpose, and work, particularly in the work of creation and salvation. Each person of the Trinity has a distinct role, yet they operate in perfect harmony, reflecting the fullness of God's love, grace, and power.

For believers, understanding the unity of the Trinity deepens our relationship with God, enriches our worship, and calls us to live in unity with one another. As we reflect on the unity of the Trinity, we are reminded of the mystery and majesty of God, who has revealed Himself to us as Father, Son, and Holy Spirit, inviting us into a relationship with Him that is rooted in love, unity, and eternal life.

CHAPTER 06

THE RESURRECTION AS THE ULTIMATE PROOF OF DIVINITY

The Power of the Resurrection: How Jesus' Resurrection Confirms His Divine Nature

16.1 Introduction

The resurrection of Jesus Christ is the cornerstone of the Christian faith. It is not only a miraculous event but also the ultimate proof of Jesus' divine nature. The resurrection demonstrates Jesus' victory over death, affirms His identity as the Son of God, and serves as the foundation for the hope of eternal life for all believers. In this chapter, we will explore how the resurrection confirms Jesus' divinity through a detailed expository study, using Bible verses, an exhaustive Strong's Concordance, and comprehensive commentary.

16.2 The Resurrection in the New Testament: A Biblical Overview

The resurrection of Jesus is a central theme throughout the New Testament, with numerous references to its significance and implications for the Christian faith. The Gospels, Acts, the Epistles, and Revelation all attest to the reality of the resurrection and its role in confirming Jesus' divine nature.

16.2.1 The Gospel Accounts of the Resurrection

Each of the four Gospels—Matthew, Mark, Luke, and John—provides an account of the resurrection. These accounts, while varying in detail, all agree on the fundamental facts: Jesus was crucified, buried, and on the third day, He rose from the dead.

- Matthew 28:5-7: "But the angel answered and said to the women, 'Do not be afraid, for I know that you seek Jesus who was crucified. He is not here; for He is risen, as He said. Come, see the place where the Lord lay. And go quickly and tell His disciples that He is risen from the dead, and indeed He is going before you into Galilee; there you will see Him. Behold, I have told you.'"

- Mark 16:6: "But he said to them, 'Do not be alarmed. You seek Jesus of Nazareth, who was crucified. He is risen! He is not here. See the place where they laid Him.'"

- Luke 24:5-7: "Then, as they were afraid and bowed their faces to the earth, they said to them, 'Why do you seek the living among the dead? He is not here, but is risen! Remember how He spoke to you when He was still in Galilee, saying, "The Son of Man must be delivered into the hands of sinful men, and be crucified, and the third day rise again."'"

- John 20:19-20: "Then, the same day at evening, being the first day of the week, when the doors were shut where the disciples were assembled, for fear of the Jews, Jesus came and stood in the midst, and said to them, 'Peace be with you.' When He had said this, He showed them His hands and His side. Then the disciples were glad when they saw the Lord."

These accounts emphasize the physical reality of Jesus' resurrection, with the empty tomb and the appearances of the risen Christ serving as irrefutable evidence of His victory over death.

16.2.2 The Resurrection in Acts

The book of Acts records the early Church's proclamation of the resurrection as central to the Gospel message. Peter's sermon on the day of Pentecost is particularly significant in highlighting the resurrection as proof of Jesus' divine identity.

- Acts 2:22-24, 32: "Men of Israel, hear these words: Jesus of Nazareth, a Man attested by God to you by miracles, wonders, and signs which God did through Him in your midst, as you yourselves also know—Him, being delivered by the determined purpose and foreknowledge of God, you have taken by lawless hands, have crucified, and put to death; whom God raised up, having loosed the pains of death, because it was not possible that He should be held by it... This Jesus God has raised up, of which we are all witnesses."

Peter's declaration that "it was not possible that He should be held by [death]" underscores the power of the resurrection as a divine act that confirms Jesus' identity as the Son of God.

16.2.3 The Resurrection in the Epistles

The apostle Paul provides a theological exposition of the resurrection in his epistles, particularly in 1 Corinthians 15, where he outlines the significance of the resurrection for the Christian faith.

- 1 Corinthians 15:3-4, 20-22: "For I delivered to you first of all that which I also received: that Christ died for our sins according to the Scriptures, and that He was buried, and that He rose again the third day according to the Scriptures... But now Christ is risen from the dead, and has become the firstfruits of those who have fallen asleep. For since by man came death, by Man also came the resurrection of the dead.

For as in Adam all die, even so in Christ all shall be made alive."

Paul's use of the term "firstfruits" (Strong's G536) refers to the first portion of the harvest, which is a pledge of the full harvest to come. By calling Jesus the firstfruits of those who have died, Paul indicates that Jesus' resurrection is the guarantee of the future resurrection of all believers.

16.2.4 The Resurrection in Revelation

The book of Revelation, written by the apostle John, also testifies to the resurrection of Jesus as the ultimate proof of His divine authority and power.

- Revelation 1:17-18: "And when I saw Him, I fell at His feet as dead. But He laid His right hand on me, saying to me, 'Do not be afraid; I am the First and the Last. I am He who lives, and was dead, and behold, I am alive forevermore. Amen. And I have the keys of Hades and of Death.'"

Jesus' declaration that He is "alive forevermore" and holds "the keys of Hades and of Death" is a powerful affirmation of His authority over life and death, rooted in His resurrection.

16.3 The Power of the Resurrection: Expository Study

To understand how the resurrection confirms Jesus' divine nature, it is essential to examine the key Greek terms used in the New Testament to describe the resurrection and the theological implications of these terms.

16.3.1 The Greek Term "Anastasis"

The Greek word for "resurrection" is "anastasis" (Strong's G386), which literally means "a standing up again" or "a raising up." This term is used throughout the New Testament to refer to both the resurrection of Jesus and the future resurrection of believers.

- 1 Corinthians 15:12-14: "Now if Christ is preached that He has been raised (anastasis) from the dead, how do some among you say that there is no resurrection (anastasis) of the dead? But if there is no resurrection (anastasis) of the dead, then Christ is not risen. And if Christ is not risen, then our preaching is empty and your faith is also empty."

Paul's argument in this passage hinges on the reality of the resurrection. The use of "anastasis" emphasizes that the resurrection is not merely a spiritual or metaphorical event but a physical, bodily raising up, affirming Jesus' victory over death.

16.3.2 The Greek Term "Egeiro"

Another important Greek term related to the resurrection is "egeiro" (Strong's G1453), which means "to awaken" or "to raise up." This term is often used in conjunction with "anastasis" to describe the act of God raising Jesus from the dead.

- Romans 4:24-25: "It shall be imputed to us who believe in Him who raised up (egeiro) Jesus our Lord from the dead, who was delivered up because of our offenses, and was raised (egeiro) because of our justification."

In this passage, Paul connects the resurrection ("egeiro") of Jesus to the believer's justification. The resurrection is not only proof of Jesus' divinity but also the basis for the believer's right standing before God.

16.3.3 Theological Implications of the Resurrection

The resurrection has profound theological implications, particularly concerning the nature of Jesus' divinity and the believer's relationship with God.

- Confirmation of Jesus' Divine Sonship: The resurrection is the ultimate confirmation of Jesus' identity as the Son of God. In Romans 1:4, Paul writes that Jesus was "declared to be the Son of God with power according to the Spirit of holiness, by the resurrection from the dead." The resurrection serves as God's public declaration that Jesus is indeed His Son, possessing the same divine nature as the Father.

- Victory Over Sin and Death: The resurrection is also the definitive proof of Jesus' victory over sin and death. In 1

Corinthians 15:54-57, Paul proclaims, "Death is swallowed up in victory. O Death, where is your sting? O Hades, where is your victory? The sting of death is sin, and the strength of sin is the law. But thanks be to God, who gives us the victory through our Lord Jesus Christ." The resurrection demonstrates that Jesus has conquered the power of sin and death, securing eternal life for all who believe in Him.

- The Hope of Resurrection for Believers: Finally, the resurrection of Jesus is the foundation for the believer's hope of resurrection. In Philippians 3:20-21, Paul writes, "For our citizenship is in heaven, from which we also eagerly wait for the Savior, the Lord Jesus Christ, who will transform our lowly body that it may be conformed to His glorious body, according to the working by which He is able even to subdue all things to Himself." The resurrection of Jesus assures believers that they too will be raised to eternal life, with transformed bodies like His.

16.4 The Resurrection as the Ultimate Proof of Divinity: Comprehensive Commentary

The resurrection of Jesus is not only a historical event but also the ultimate proof of His divine nature. This truth is affirmed by the unanimous testimony of the New Testament writers and is central to Christian doctrine.

16.4.1 Historical Evidence for the Resurrection

The resurrection is one of the most well-attested events in ancient history. The empty tomb, the post-resurrection appearances of Jesus, and the transformation of the apostles from fearful followers to bold proclaimers of the Gospel all point to the reality of the resurrection.

- The Empty Tomb: All four Gospels agree that Jesus' tomb was found empty on the third day after His crucifixion. The fact that the tomb was empty is significant because it means that Jesus' body was not stolen or misplaced but was raised by the power of God.

- Post-Resurrection Appearances: The risen Jesus appeared to many people over a period of forty days, including Mary Magdalene, the apostles, and more than five hundred brethren at once (1 Corinthians 15:6). These appearances were physical and tangible, as Jesus invited His disciples to touch His wounds and ate with them (Luke 24:39-43).

- The Transformation of the Apostles: The apostles, who had fled in fear after Jesus' arrest, were transformed into fearless witnesses of the resurrection after encountering the risen Christ. This dramatic change in their behavior is best explained by the reality of the resurrection.

16.4.2 Theological Significance of the Resurrection

The resurrection is not only the ultimate proof of Jesus' divinity but also the foundation of Christian theology. Without the resurrection, there would be no Gospel, no salvation, and no hope of eternal life.

- The Foundation of the Gospel: In 1 Corinthians 15:14, Paul states, "And if Christ is not risen, then our preaching is empty and your faith is also empty." The resurrection is the cornerstone of the Gospel message, affirming that Jesus' death on the cross was effective in atoning for sin and that His promise of eternal life is true.

- The Basis for Justification: The resurrection is also the basis for the believer's justification. In Romans 4:25, Paul writes that Jesus "was raised because of our justification." The resurrection confirms that Jesus' sacrifice was accepted by God and that believers are declared righteous through faith in Him.

- The Hope of Eternal Life: Finally, the resurrection is the foundation of the believer's hope of eternal life. In 1 Peter 1:3-4, Peter writes, "Blessed be the God and Father of our Lord Jesus Christ, who according to His abundant mercy has begotten us again to a living hope through the resurrection of Jesus Christ from the dead, to an inheritance incorruptible and undefiled and that does not fade away, reserved in heaven for you." The resurrection assures believers that they will share in the same victory over death that Jesus achieved.

16.4.3 The Resurrection and the Trinity

The resurrection of Jesus is also a profound demonstration of the unity and power of the Trinity. The Father, Son, and Holy Spirit all played a role in the resurrection, highlighting the cooperative work of the Godhead in accomplishing redemption.

- The Father: The New Testament frequently attributes the resurrection to the power of God the Father. In Romans 6:4, Paul writes, "Therefore we were buried with Him through baptism into death, that just as Christ was raised from the dead by the glory of the Father, even so we also should walk in newness of life." The Father's role in raising Jesus confirms His approval of the Son's sacrifice and His authority over life and death.

- The Son: Jesus Himself predicted His resurrection and demonstrated His divine authority by rising from the dead. In John 10:17-18, Jesus says, "Therefore My Father loves Me, because I lay down My life that I may take it again. No one takes it from Me, but I lay it down of Myself. I have power to lay it down, and I have power to take it again. This command I have received from My Father." Jesus' resurrection is a self-affirming act that reveals His sovereignty and divinity.

- The Holy Spirit: The Holy Spirit is also intimately involved in the resurrection. In Romans 8:11, Paul states, "But if the Spirit of Him who raised Jesus from the dead dwells in you, He who raised Christ from the dead will also give life to your mortal bodies through His Spirit who dwells in you." The Spirit's role in the resurrection highlights the power and unity of the Godhead in bringing about the victory over death.

16.5 Conclusion

The resurrection of Jesus Christ is the ultimate proof of His divine nature. It confirms His identity as the Son of God, demonstrates His victory over sin and death, and provides the foundation for the believer's hope of eternal life. The resurrection is attested by the unanimous testimony of the New Testament, supported by historical evidence, and affirmed by the cooperative work of the Trinity.

As believers, we are called to live in the light of the resurrection, recognizing Jesus' divine authority and trusting in the promise of eternal life that He has secured for us. The power of the resurrection is not only a past event but a present reality that continues to transform lives and empower the Church to proclaim the Gospel to the ends of the earth.

In the words of the apostle Paul, "Thanks be to God, who gives us the victory through our Lord Jesus Christ" (1 Corinthians 15:57). The resurrection is the ultimate declaration of that victory, a victory that confirms Jesus as the divine Son of God and the Savior of the world.

The Role of the Holy Spirit in the Resurrection

The Spirit's Involvement in Raising Jesus from the Dead (Romans 8:11)

17.1 Introduction

The resurrection of Jesus Christ is the pivotal event in Christian theology, affirming His victory over sin and death and confirming His identity as the Son of God. While the resurrection is often associated with the power and authority of God the Father, the New Testament also highlights the significant role of the Holy Spirit in this event. In Romans 8:11, the apostle Paul specifically mentions the involvement of the Holy Spirit in raising Jesus from the dead. This chapter will explore the role of the Holy Spirit in the resurrection, drawing on biblical references, an expository study using Strong's Concordance, and comprehensive commentary to understand the theological significance of the Spirit's involvement.

17.2 Romans 8:11: The Holy Spirit and the Resurrection

Romans 8:11 is a key verse that explicitly connects the Holy Spirit with the resurrection of Jesus Christ:

- Romans 8:11 (NKJV): "But if the Spirit of Him who raised Jesus from the dead dwells in you, He who raised Christ from the dead will also give life to your mortal bodies through His Spirit who dwells in you."

This verse not only affirms the Spirit's role in raising Jesus but also extends the promise of resurrection life to all believers, emphasizing the ongoing work of the Holy Spirit in the lives of those who follow Christ.

17.2.1 Exegesis of Romans 8:11

To fully understand the meaning and implications of Romans 8:11, we must examine the key terms used in the original Greek language, with the aid of Strong's Concordance:

- "Spirit" (πνεῦμα, pneuma - Strong's G4151): The term "pneuma" refers to the Holy Spirit, the third person of the Trinity, who is characterized by divine power and presence. In this context, the Spirit is the agent of resurrection, demonstrating the power of God in raising Jesus from the dead.

- "Raised" (ἐγείρω, egeiro - Strong's G1453): The verb "egeiro" means "to awaken" or "to raise up." This term is commonly used in the New Testament to describe the act of God raising Jesus from the dead. The use of "egeiro" here emphasizes the active role of the Holy Spirit in bringing Jesus back to life.

- "Dwells" (οἰκέω, oikeo - Strong's G3611): The verb "oikeo" means "to inhabit" or "to live in." This term is used to describe the indwelling presence of the Holy Spirit in believers, indicating that the same Spirit who raised Jesus now resides within those who belong to Christ.

- "Give life" (ζῳοποιέω, zoopoieo - Strong's G2227): The verb "zoopoieo" means "to make alive" or "to quicken." This term highlights the life-giving power of the Holy Spirit, who not only raised Jesus but also imparts resurrection life to believers.

Paul's use of these terms underscores the transformative power of the Holy Spirit, both in the resurrection of Jesus and in the ongoing spiritual renewal of believers.

17.2.2 The Theological Implications of Romans 8:11

Romans 8:11 carries significant theological implications regarding the role of the Holy Spirit in the resurrection:

- Affirmation of the Spirit's Divine Power: The verse affirms the divine power of the Holy Spirit, equating the Spirit's work in the resurrection with the life-giving power of God. The Spirit is not a mere force or influence but a divine person who actively participates in the most crucial events of redemptive history.

- Connection Between Christ's Resurrection and Believers' Resurrection: Paul's statement links the resurrection of Jesus with the future resurrection of believers. The same Spirit who raised Jesus from the dead will also give life to the mortal bodies of believers, assuring them of their future resurrection and eternal life.

- Indwelling Presence of the Spirit: The verse emphasizes the indwelling presence of the Holy Spirit in believers. This indwelling is not passive but actively involved in imparting life, both now and in the resurrection to come. The Spirit's presence within believers is a guarantee of their future resurrection.

17.3 The Holy Spirit in the New Testament: The Spirit's Role in the Resurrection

The involvement of the Holy Spirit in the resurrection of Jesus is a theme that is woven throughout the New Testament. Various passages highlight the Spirit's role, not only in raising Jesus but also in the broader context of the resurrection and the life-giving work of the Spirit.

17.3.1 The Spirit as the Agent of Resurrection

The New Testament presents the Holy Spirit as the divine agent through whom the resurrection of Jesus was accomplished. This role is integral to the Spirit's identity and work within the Godhead.

- Romans 1:4: "And declared to be the Son of God with power according to the Spirit of holiness, by the resurrection from the dead: Jesus Christ our Lord."

In this verse, Paul emphasizes that Jesus was declared to be the Son of God with power through the resurrection, which was accomplished "according to the Spirit of holiness." The term "Spirit of holiness" here underscores the Holy Spirit's sanctifying and life-giving power, which validated Jesus' divine sonship through the resurrection.

- 1 Peter 3:18: "For Christ also suffered once for sins, the just for the unjust, that He might bring us to God, being put to death in the flesh but made alive by the Spirit."

Peter affirms that Jesus was "made alive by the Spirit," indicating that the Holy Spirit played a direct role in bringing Jesus back to life. This resurrection was not just a physical revival but a powerful vindication of Jesus' righteous sacrifice, achieved through the Spirit's life-giving power.

17.3.2 The Spirit's Role in the Life and Ministry of Jesus

The Holy Spirit's involvement in Jesus' resurrection is part of a broader pattern of the Spirit's work throughout Jesus' life and ministry.

- Conception of Jesus: The Holy Spirit was involved from the very beginning of Jesus' earthly life. Luke 1:35 records the angel Gabriel's words to Mary: "The Holy Spirit will come upon you, and the power of the Highest will overshadow you; therefore, also, that Holy One who is to be born will be called the Son of God." The Spirit's role in the conception of Jesus set the stage for His divine mission, which would culminate in the resurrection.

- Baptism and Anointing: At Jesus' baptism, the Holy Spirit descended upon Him in the form of a dove (Matthew 3:16). This anointing by the Spirit empowered Jesus for His public ministry, including His miracles, teachings, and ultimately, His sacrificial death and resurrection. The Spirit's presence throughout Jesus' ministry affirmed His divine identity and mission.

- Empowerment for Ministry: Jesus performed His miracles and proclaimed the kingdom of God through the power of the Holy Spirit. In Matthew 12:28, Jesus says, "But if I cast out demons by the Spirit of God, surely the kingdom of God has come upon you." The Spirit's empowerment of Jesus demonstrated His authority over evil and His role as the bringer of God's kingdom, leading to the ultimate victory in the resurrection.

17.3.3 The Holy Spirit and the Resurrection Life of Believers

The role of the Holy Spirit in Jesus' resurrection has direct implications for the life of believers. The Spirit who raised Jesus from the dead is also at work in those who follow Christ, empowering them to live in the reality of the resurrection.

- Ephesians 1:19-20: "And what is the exceeding greatness of His power toward us who believe, according to the working of His mighty power which He worked in Christ when He raised Him from the dead and seated Him at His right hand in the heavenly places."

Paul emphasizes that the same power that raised Jesus from the dead is at work in believers. This "mighty power" (Greek: "dynamis," Strong's G1411) is a reference to the Holy Spirit, whose life-giving presence empowers believers to live victorious lives in Christ.

- 2 Corinthians 4:14: "Knowing that He who raised up the Lord Jesus will also raise us up with Jesus, and will present us with you."

The Holy Spirit's role in raising Jesus is the guarantee of the future resurrection of believers. Just as the Spirit raised Jesus, so will He raise those who belong to Him, presenting them blameless before the Father.

- Romans 6:4: "Therefore we were buried with Him through baptism into death, that just as Christ was raised from the dead by the glory of the Father, even so we also should walk in newness of life."

While this verse primarily attributes the resurrection to "the glory of the Father," it is understood within the broader Trinitarian context that the Holy Spirit was actively involved in this "glory." The Spirit's work in believers is to enable them to "walk in newness of life," living out the resurrection power that was demonstrated in Jesus.

17.4 Comprehensive Commentary on the Holy Spirit's Role in the Resurrection

The role of the Holy Spirit in the resurrection is integral to understanding the full scope of the Trinity's work in redemption. The Holy Spirit's involvement highlights the cooperative nature of the Godhead and the Spirit's unique contribution to bringing about new life.

17.4.1 The Cooperative Work of the Trinity

The resurrection of

Jesus is a Trinitarian event, with the Father, Son, and Holy Spirit all participating in bringing about this decisive moment in redemptive history. The Father's will, the Son's obedience, and the Spirit's power are all essential components of the resurrection.

- The Father's Role: The Father is often depicted as the one who raises Jesus from the dead. Acts 2:24 states, "Whom God raised up, having loosed the pains of death, because it was not possible that He should be held by it." The Father's action in the resurrection is an affirmation of His approval of the Son's sacrifice and a demonstration of His authority over death.

- The Son's Role: Jesus, as the Son, willingly lays down His life and takes it up again, as He declares in John 10:17-18. The resurrection is both an act of the Father raising the Son and the Son exercising His own divine authority to overcome death.

- The Spirit's Role: The Holy Spirit, as the life-giver, is the one who empowers the resurrection, applying the power of God to raise Jesus from the dead. The Spirit's role in the resurrection is a manifestation of His life-giving nature, which is also at work in the spiritual and future physical resurrection of believers.

The cooperative work of the Trinity in the resurrection reveals the unity and diversity within the Godhead, where each person of the Trinity contributes to the accomplishment of God's redemptive plan.

17.4.2 The Spirit as the Giver of Life

The Holy Spirit is often referred to as the "Giver of Life," a title that reflects His role in creation, regeneration, and resurrection. The Spirit's life-giving power is evident in the resurrection of Jesus, where He breathes new life into the crucified body of Christ, restoring Him to glorified, eternal life.

- Genesis 2:7: "And the Lord God formed man of the dust of the ground, and breathed into his nostrils the breath of life; and man became a living being."

The same Spirit who breathed life into Adam is the one who breathes life into the dead body of Jesus, raising Him to new life. This creative power of the Spirit is also at work in the new creation, where believers are made alive in Christ through the Spirit.

- John 6:63: "It is the Spirit who gives life; the flesh profits nothing. The words that I speak to you are spirit, and they are life."

Jesus Himself emphasizes that it is the Spirit who gives life. This life-giving work of the Spirit is fully realized in the resurrection, where the Spirit raises Jesus and, by extension, guarantees the resurrection life of all who are in Him.

17.4.3 The Spirit's Indwelling as the Guarantee of Resurrection

One of the most significant aspects of the Holy Spirit's role in the resurrection is His indwelling presence in believers. The Spirit's indwelling is described as a "seal" and a "guarantee" (Greek: "arrabon," Strong's G728) of the believer's future resurrection.

- 2 Corinthians 1:21-22: "Now He who establishes us with you in Christ and has anointed us is God, who also has sealed us and given us the Spirit in our hearts as a guarantee."

The Spirit's indwelling presence is a down payment, assuring believers that they will be raised with Christ. This guarantee is not just a promise of future resurrection but also the present experience of resurrection life through the Spirit's work in sanctification and spiritual renewal.

- Ephesians 1:13-14: "In Him you also trusted, after you heard the word of truth, the gospel of your salvation; in whom also, having believed, you were sealed with the Holy Spirit of promise, who is the guarantee of our inheritance until the redemption of the purchased possession, to the praise of His glory."

The Holy Spirit is the "seal" of the believer's inheritance, confirming that they belong to God and will share in the resurrection life of Christ. This sealing by the Spirit is both a sign of ownership and a pledge of the future fulfillment of God's promises.

17.5 Conclusion

The role of the Holy Spirit in the resurrection of Jesus is a profound demonstration of the Spirit's divine power and life-giving nature. Romans 8:11 encapsulates this truth, revealing that the same Spirit who raised Jesus from the dead now dwells in believers, assuring them of their future resurrection and empowering them to live in the reality of Christ's victory over death.

The resurrection is a Trinitarian event, with the Holy Spirit playing a crucial role in bringing Jesus back to life and in securing the believer's hope of eternal life. The Spirit's involvement in the resurrection highlights the unity of the Godhead and the Spirit's ongoing work in applying the benefits of Christ's resurrection to the lives of believers.

As we reflect on the Holy Spirit's role in the resurrection, we are reminded of the transformative power of the Spirit in our own lives. The Spirit not only raised Jesus from the dead but also raises us to new life in Christ, empowering us to live as resurrected people who walk in the newness of life. The Spirit's indwelling presence is a guarantee of our future resurrection and a source of strength and hope as we await the full realization of God's promises in the age to come.

Jesus' Appearances and Ascension

How the Resurrection Appearances and Ascension Further Demonstrate His Divinity

18.1 Introduction

The resurrection of Jesus Christ is the pivotal event that confirms His divinity, but it is not the only event that does so. The appearances of the risen Christ to His disciples and others, as well as His ascension into heaven, are further demonstrations of His divine nature. These events not only validate the reality of the resurrection but also reveal important aspects of Jesus' divine identity and mission. In this chapter, we will explore how Jesus' resurrection appearances and His ascension serve as powerful affirmations of His divinity, using biblical references and comprehensive commentary.

18.2 The Resurrection Appearances: Affirming Jesus' Divinity

The New Testament records multiple appearances of Jesus after His resurrection, each serving to affirm His divinity and reinforce the truth of His victory over death. These appearances are not merely incidental; they are central to the Christian proclamation of the risen Lord.

18.2.1 The First Appearances: The Women at the Tomb

The first witnesses to the resurrection were women who visited Jesus' tomb early on the first day of the week. The Gospels emphasize the significance of these appearances, particularly in a cultural context where the testimony of women was often undervalued.

- Matthew 28:9-10: "And as they went to tell His disciples, behold, Jesus met them, saying, 'Rejoice!' So they came and held Him by the feet and worshiped Him. Then Jesus said to them, 'Do not be afraid. Go and tell My brethren to go to Galilee, and there they will see Me.'"

In this appearance, Jesus not only comforts the women but also commissions them to announce His resurrection to the disciples. The fact that they "worshiped Him" (Greek: προσκυνέω, proskuneo - Strong's G4352) is significant, as worship is an act reserved for God alone. This response to Jesus' appearance affirms His divinity.

18.2.2 The Appearance to Mary Magdalene

Mary Magdalene's encounter with the risen Jesus is one of the most intimate and personal of the resurrection appearances. It highlights both the reality of the resurrection and Jesus' divine authority.

- John 20:16-18: "Jesus said to her, 'Mary!' She turned and said to Him, 'Rabboni!' (which is to say, Teacher). Jesus said to her, 'Do not cling to Me, for I have not yet ascended to My Father; but go to My brethren and say to them, "I am ascending to My Father and your Father, and to My God and your God."' Mary Magdalene came and told the disciples that she had seen the Lord, and that He had spoken these things to her."

In this encounter, Jesus' personal address to Mary by name and her immediate recognition of Him as "Rabboni" reflects His intimate knowledge and divine authority. His instruction not to cling to Him because He has not yet ascended points to the significance of the upcoming ascension, which will further demonstrate His divine nature and mission.

18.2.3 The Appearance to the Disciples on the Road to Emmaus

One of the most profound post-resurrection appearances is Jesus' encounter with two disciples on the road to Emmaus. This appearance emphasizes Jesus' role as the fulfillment of Scripture and His divine ability to reveal Himself to His followers.

- Luke 24:30-32: "Now it came to pass, as He sat at the table with them, that He took bread, blessed and broke it, and gave it to them. Then their eyes were opened and they knew Him; and He vanished from their sight. And they said to one another, 'Did not our heart burn within us while He talked with us on the road, and while He opened the Scriptures to us?'"

Jesus' breaking of bread with the disciples, reminiscent of the Last Supper, leads to the moment of revelation where they recognize Him. His sudden vanishing emphasizes His divine nature, transcending the normal limitations of the human body. Furthermore, His ability to "open the Scriptures" points to His divine wisdom and authority as the fulfillment of the Law and the Prophets.

18.2.4 The Appearance to Thomas

The appearance to Thomas is particularly significant in affirming Jesus' divinity, as it directly addresses doubt and leads to one of the clearest confessions of Jesus' divine identity.

- John 20:27-29: "Then He said to Thomas, 'Reach your finger here, and look at My hands; and reach your hand here, and put it into My side. Do not be unbelieving, but believing.' And Thomas answered and said to Him, 'My Lord and my God!' Jesus said to him, 'Thomas, because you have seen Me, you have believed. Blessed are those who have not seen and yet have believed.'"

Thomas' declaration, "My Lord and my God!" (Greek: Ὁ Κύριός μου καὶ Ὁ Θεός μου, Ho Kyrios mou kai Ho Theos mou), is one of the most explicit affirmations of Jesus' divinity in the New Testament. Jesus does not rebuke Thomas for this confession but rather blesses it, thereby affirming His identity as both Lord and God.

18.2.5 The Appearance to the Disciples by the Sea of Galilee

Jesus' appearance to His disciples by the Sea of Galilee further demonstrates His divinity through a miraculous provision and a reaffirmation of Peter's role in the Church.

- John 21:6-7: "And He said to them, 'Cast the net on the right side of the boat, and you will find some.' So they cast, and now they were not able to draw it in because of the multitude of fish. Therefore that disciple whom Jesus loved said to Peter, 'It is the Lord!' Now when Simon Peter heard that it was the Lord, he put on his outer garment (for he had removed it), and plunged into the sea."

The miraculous catch of fish is reminiscent of Jesus' earlier miracles and serves as a divine sign that the risen Christ is the same Lord who performed wonders during His earthly ministry. The recognition of Jesus as "the Lord" by the disciples further confirms His divine identity.

18.3 The Ascension: The Ultimate Demonstration of Jesus' Divinity

The ascension of Jesus into heaven is a climactic event that not only concludes His earthly ministry but also provides definitive proof of His divinity. The ascension is recorded in both Luke's Gospel and the Acts of the Apostles, and it is alluded to in other New Testament writings.

18.3.1 The Ascension as the Exaltation of Jesus

The ascension is not merely a departure from earth but an exaltation of Jesus to the right hand of God, a position of supreme authority and power.

- Luke 24:50-51: "And He led them out as far as Bethany, and He lifted up His hands and blessed them. Now it came to pass, while He blessed them, that He was parted from them and carried up into heaven."

- Acts 1:9-11: "Now when He had spoken these things, while they watched, He was taken up, and a cloud received Him out of their sight. And while they looked steadfastly toward heaven as He went up, behold, two men stood by them in white apparel, who also said, 'Men of Galilee, why do you stand gazing up into heaven? This same

Jesus, who was taken up from you into heaven, will so come in like manner as you saw Him go into heaven.'"

In both accounts, the ascension is portrayed as a supernatural event, with Jesus being "carried up" or "taken up" into heaven, demonstrating His divine nature. The cloud that receives Him is often interpreted as the Shekinah glory of God, further emphasizing His divine status.

18.3.2 The Ascension and the Right Hand of God

The New Testament frequently refers to Jesus being seated at the right hand of God following His ascension. This position signifies both honor and authority, underscoring Jesus' divinity and His role as the sovereign ruler of all creation.

- Hebrews 1:3: "Who being the brightness of His glory and the express image of His person, and upholding all things by the word of His power, when He had by Himself purged our sins, sat down at the right hand of the Majesty on high."

- Ephesians 1:20-21: "Which He worked in Christ when He raised Him from the dead and seated Him at His right hand in the heavenly places, far above all principality and power and might and dominion, and every name that is named, not only in this age but also in that which is to come."

The ascension and subsequent enthronement at the right hand of God confirm Jesus' divine authority over all powers and dominions. His position "far above all principality and power" indicates that He shares in the divine sovereignty of God the Father.

18.3.3 The Ascension as the Precursor to the Sending of the Holy Spirit

The ascension is also significant because it precedes the sending of the Holy Spirit at Pentecost. Jesus Himself indicated that His departure was necessary for the Holy Spirit to come.

- John 16:7: "Nevertheless I tell you the truth. It is to your advantage that I go away; for if I do not go away, the Helper will not come to you; but if I depart, I will send Him to you."

The sending of the Holy Spirit is a continuation of Jesus' divine mission and a further demonstration of His authority. The Holy Spirit, proceeding from the Father and the Son, testifies to Jesus' divinity by empowering the Church and enabling believers to carry out His mission on earth.

18.3.4 The Ascension and the Promise of Jesus' Return

The ascension is also closely linked to the promise of Jesus' return, which is a key element of Christian eschatology.

The angels' message in Acts 1:11 assures the disciples that "this same Jesus" will return in the same manner as He ascended, affirming the continuity of His divine mission.

- Acts 1:11: "'Men of Galilee, why do you stand gazing up into heaven? This same Jesus, who was taken up from you into heaven, will so come in like manner as you saw Him go into heaven.'"

The promise of Jesus' return underscores His ongoing divine authority and the fulfillment of God's redemptive plan. The ascension, therefore, is not the end of Jesus' work but a transition to a new phase of His divine mission, which will culminate in His second coming.

18.4 Theological Implications of the Resurrection Appearances and Ascension

The resurrection appearances and ascension of Jesus are not merely historical events but carry profound theological implications that affirm His divinity and shape Christian belief and practice.

18.4.1 The Validation of Jesus' Claims

The resurrection appearances and ascension validate Jesus' claims about His identity and mission. Throughout His ministry, Jesus made bold claims about His relationship with the Father, His authority to forgive sins, and His role as the Son of God. The resurrection and ascension serve as divine endorsements of these claims, confirming that Jesus is who He said He was.

- John 14:6: "Jesus said to him, 'I am the way, the truth, and the life. No one comes to the Father except through Me.'"

The resurrection and ascension affirm that Jesus is indeed "the way, the truth, and the life," and that His teachings and claims are divinely authenticated.

18.4.2 The Basis for Christian Worship

The resurrection appearances, where Jesus is worshiped by His followers, and the ascension, where He is exalted to the right hand of God, provide the foundation for Christian worship. The early Church's practice of worshiping Jesus as Lord (Greek: Κύριος, Kyrios) is rooted in these events.

- Philippians 2:9-11: "Therefore God also has highly exalted Him and given Him the name which is above every name, that at the name of Jesus every knee should bow, of those in heaven, and of those on earth, and of those under the earth, and that every tongue should confess that Jesus Christ is Lord, to the glory of God the Father."

The worship of Jesus as Lord is a direct response to His resurrection and ascension, which reveal His divine nature and authority. This worship is not idolatry but is appropriate because Jesus shares in the divine identity of the Father.

18.4.3 The Role of Jesus as Mediator and Intercessor

The ascension also highlights Jesus' ongoing role as the mediator and intercessor for believers. Seated at the right hand of God, Jesus continues to intercede on behalf of His followers, ensuring their salvation and sanctification.

- Hebrews 7:25: "Therefore He is also able to save to the uttermost those who come to God through Him, since He always lives to make intercession for them."

Jesus' role as intercessor underscores His divine nature, as He occupies a position of unique authority and closeness to the Father. His ascension and ongoing intercession provide believers with confidence in their salvation and access to God's grace.

18.4.4 The Empowerment of the Church

The ascension is also significant because it leads to the empowerment of the Church through the Holy Spirit. Jesus' promise to send the Holy Spirit after His ascension is fulfilled at Pentecost, marking the beginning of the Church's mission to spread the Gospel to the ends of the earth.

- Acts 2:32-33: "This Jesus God has raised up, of which we are all witnesses. Therefore being exalted to the right hand of God, and having received from the Father the promise of the Holy Spirit, He poured out this which you now see and hear."

The outpouring of the Holy Spirit is a direct result of Jesus' ascension, confirming His divine authority to empower His followers for ministry. The Spirit's presence in the Church is a continuation of Jesus' divine mission, demonstrating that He remains active and sovereign over His people.

18.5 Conclusion

The resurrection appearances and ascension of Jesus Christ are powerful demonstrations of His divinity. The appearances validate the reality of the resurrection, reveal Jesus' divine nature, and provide the foundation for the Christian faith. The ascension, as the climax of Jesus' earthly ministry, affirms His exaltation to the right hand of God and His ongoing role as Lord, mediator, and intercessor.

These events are not only historical occurrences but also theological affirmations that shape the worship, mission, and hope of the Church. The resurrection appearances and ascension remind believers that Jesus is both fully divine and fully human, victorious over death, and sovereign over all creation.

As the Church continues to proclaim the risen and ascended Lord, it does so with the assurance that Jesus is who He claimed to be—the Son of God, the Savior of the world, and the King of kings. This proclamation is rooted in the reality of the resurrection and ascension, which together provide irrefutable evidence of Jesus' divinity and the truth of the Christian Gospel.

CHAPTER 07

THE IMPLICATIONS OF JESUS'S DIVINITY FOR BELIEVERS

Salvation Through Christ: Why Only a Divine Savior Can Offer Salvation

19.1 Introduction

The doctrine of salvation lies at the heart of the Christian faith. It is the belief that through Jesus Christ, humanity is offered redemption from sin and the promise of eternal life. However, this salvation is not merely the work of a great teacher, prophet, or moral leader. It is the work of God Himself, accomplished through Jesus Christ, who is fully divine and fully human. The divinity of Christ is essential to the Christian understanding of salvation. Only a divine Savior could bear the weight of the world's sin, satisfy the demands of divine justice, and offer redemption to all who believe. In this chapter, we will explore why only a divine Savior can offer salvation, examining the theological and biblical foundations that underscore this truth.

19.2 The Nature of Sin and the Need for a Divine Savior

To understand why only a divine Savior can offer salvation, it is essential first to grasp the nature of sin and the separation it causes between humanity and God. Sin is not merely a moral failing; it is a profound rebellion against the holy and righteous nature of God. The Bible teaches that all humans are born in sin and are incapable of saving themselves through their own efforts.

19.2.1 The Universality of Sin

The Bible consistently affirms that all have sinned and fall short of the glory of God. This universal condition of sin is the root of humanity's need for salvation.

- Romans 3:23: "For all have sinned and fall short of the glory of God."

- Isaiah 53:6: "All we like sheep have gone astray; we have turned, every one, to his own way; and the Lord has laid on Him the iniquity of us all."

Sin is a pervasive and intrinsic part of the human condition, affecting every aspect of our being. It results in spiritual death, separation from God, and the inability to fulfill

God's righteous standards. This condition cannot be remedied by human effort or good works; it requires divine intervention.

19.2.2 The Severity of Sin and Divine Justice

The seriousness of sin is rooted in the nature of God as holy and just. God's holiness means that He is utterly pure and separate from sin, while His justice demands that sin be punished.

- Habakkuk 1:13: "You are of purer eyes than to behold evil, and cannot look on wickedness."

- Romans 6:23: "For the wages of sin is death, but the gift of God is eternal life in Christ Jesus our Lord."

Because of God's perfect justice, sin must be punished. The punishment for sin is death, which means both physical death and eternal separation from God. No human being can escape this judgment on their own, as all are guilty before God. Therefore, only a Savior who is both fully divine and fully human can bridge the gap between a holy God and sinful humanity.

19.3 The Divinity of Christ: The Foundation for Salvation

The Bible teaches that Jesus Christ is both fully God and fully man. This dual nature is essential for His role as Savior. As fully God, Jesus has the power and authority to forgive sins and grant eternal life. As fully man, He is able to represent humanity and bear the penalty for sin on our behalf.

19.3.1 The Incarnation: God Becoming Man

The incarnation of Jesus Christ is the foundational truth that God became man in the person of Jesus. This act of divine condescension is the basis for our salvation.

- John 1:1, 14: "In the beginning was the Word, and the Word was with God, and the Word was God... And the Word became flesh and dwelt among us, and we beheld His glory, the glory as of the only begotten of the Father, full of grace and truth."

- Philippians 2:6-8: "Who, being in the form of God, did not consider it robbery to be equal with God, but made Himself of no reputation, taking the form of a bondservant, and coming in the likeness of men. And being found in appearance as a man, He humbled Himself and became obedient to the point of death, even the death of the cross."

In the incarnation, God the Son took on human nature without ceasing to be God. This mystery of the God-man is crucial because it means that Jesus, as both God and man, could fulfill the requirements of the Law, live a sinless life, and offer Himself as the perfect sacrifice for sin.

19.3.2 The Atonement: The Divine Sacrifice for Sin

The atonement refers to the work of Christ in reconciling humanity to God through His sacrificial death on the cross. Only a divine Savior could accomplish this work because the atonement requires a perfect and infinite sacrifice.

- Hebrews 9:14: "How much more shall the blood of Christ, who through the eternal Spirit offered Himself without spot to God, cleanse your conscience from dead works to serve the living God?"

- 1 Peter 1:18-19: "Knowing that you were not redeemed with corruptible things, like silver or gold, from your aimless conduct received by tradition from your fathers, but with the precious blood of Christ, as of a lamb without blemish and without spot."

The blood of Christ, as the divine Lamb of God, is of infinite value. It is sufficient to cover the sins of all who believe in Him. Because Jesus is divine, His sacrifice is not limited in scope or power. It is capable of atoning for the sins of the entire world, making salvation available to all who place their faith in Him.

19.3.3 The Resurrection: The Divine Victory Over Death

The resurrection of Jesus Christ is the ultimate proof of His divinity and the confirmation that His sacrifice was accepted by God. It is through the resurrection that Jesus conquers death and offers eternal life to all who believe.

- Romans 1:4: "And declared to be the Son of God with power according to the Spirit of holiness, by the resurrection from the dead: Jesus Christ our Lord."

- 1 Corinthians 15:20-22: "But now Christ is risen from the dead, and has become the firstfruits of those who have fallen asleep. For since by man came death, by Man also came the resurrection of the dead. For as in Adam all die, even so in Christ all shall be made alive."

The resurrection demonstrates that Jesus has authority over life and death, an authority that only God possesses. Because Jesus is divine, He is able to give eternal life to those who trust in Him, securing their salvation through His victory over the grave.

19.4 The Necessity of a Divine Savior for Salvation

The divinity of Christ is not just an abstract theological concept; it is essential for understanding why only He can offer salvation. There are several key reasons why a divine Savior is necessary for the salvation of humanity.

19.4.1 The Sufficiency of the Sacrifice

A central aspect of salvation is the need for a sufficient sacrifice to atone for sin. Human beings, being finite and sinful, could never offer a sacrifice that fully satisfies the demands of God's justice. Only a divine Savior, who is both infinite and sinless, could offer such a sacrifice.

- Hebrews 10:12-14: "But this Man, after He had offered one sacrifice for sins forever, sat down at the right hand of God, from that time waiting till His enemies are made His footstool. For by one offering He has perfected forever those who re being sanctified."

The sufficiency of Christ's sacrifice is rooted in His divine nature. Because He is God, His sacrifice has infinite value, able to atone for the sins of all humanity for all time. No other sacrifice could accomplish this.

19.4.2 The Authority to Forgive Sins

Forgiveness of sins is a divine prerogative. In the Gospels, Jesus frequently forgave sins, demonstrating His authority as God.

- Mark 2:5-7: "When Jesus saw their faith, He said to the paralytic, 'Son, your sins are forgiven you.' And some of the scribes were sitting there and reasoning in their hearts, 'Why does this Man speak blasphemies like this? Who can forgive sins but God alone?'"

The scribes' question underscores the truth that only God has the authority to forgive sins. By forgiving sins, Jesus was asserting His divinity. If Jesus were merely a human prophet or teacher, He would not have the authority to forgive sins. But as the divine Son of God, He has the power to forgive all who come to Him in faith.

19.4.3 The Mediator Between God and Humanity

Jesus' divinity is also essential for His role as the mediator between God and humanity. A mediator must be able to represent both parties; in this case, God and humanity. Jesus, being both fully God and fully man, is uniquely qualified to fulfill this role.

- 1 Timothy 2:5-6: "For there is one God and one Mediator between God and men, the Man Christ Jesus, who gave Himself a ransom for all, to be testified in due time."

As the divine Mediator, Jesus bridges the gap between a holy God and sinful humanity. His divinity ensures that He can fully represent God's interests and bring about reconciliation, while His humanity ensures that He can fully represent humanity's need for redemption.

19.4.4 The Source of Eternal Life

Finally, only a divine Savior can be the source of eternal life. Eternal life is not just a prolongation of existence; it is the life of God Himself, shared with those who are in Christ. Because Jesus is divine, He is the author and giver of eternal life.

- John 10:27-28: "My sheep hear My voice, and I know them, and they follow Me. And I give them eternal life, and they shall never perish; neither shall anyone snatch them out of My hand."

- John 14:6: "Jesus said to him, 'I am the way, the truth, and the life. No one comes to the Father except through Me.'"

Jesus, as the source of eternal life, offers a quality of life that only God can give. This eternal life is not merely future; it begins now for those who believe, as they are brought into a relationship with the living God through Christ.

19.5 Conclusion

The divinity of Jesus Christ is not an optional doctrine; it is essential for the Christian understanding of salvation. Only a divine Savior can offer salvation because only He can provide a sufficient sacrifice, possess the authority to forgive sins, serve as the perfect mediator between God and humanity, and be the source of eternal life.

Throughout the New Testament, the divinity of Christ is affirmed and celebrated as the foundation of the Gospel. Jesus is not merely a moral teacher or a prophet; He is God incarnate, who came to seek and save the lost. His divine nature ensures that His work of redemption is complete, effective, and available to all who place their faith in Him.

As believers, our salvation is secure not because of our own efforts or righteousness but because of who Jesus is—

the divine Savior who gave His life for us and rose again to grant us eternal life. This truth should lead us to worship, trust, and follow Him with all our hearts, knowing that in Him we have a Savior who is fully able to save us to the uttermost.

The Indwelling of the Holy Spirit

How the Holy Spirit Unites Believers with the Divine Nature of Christ

20.1 Introduction

One of the most profound truths of the Christian faith is the indwelling of the Holy Spirit in believers. This indwelling is not merely a sign of God's presence but is the means by which believers are united with the divine nature of Christ. The Holy Spirit, the third person of the Trinity, works within believers to transform them into the likeness of Christ, imparting to them the very life and nature of God. This chapter will explore how the Holy Spirit unites believers with the divine nature of Christ, examining the biblical foundation for this doctrine, its theological significance, and its practical implications for Christian living.

20.2 The Promise and Reality of the Holy Spirit's Indwelling

The indwelling of the Holy Spirit is a promise given by Jesus and fulfilled in the lives of believers. This indwelling is central to the Christian experience, as it brings about the union between the believer and Christ.

20.2.1 The Promise of the Holy Spirit

Before His crucifixion, Jesus promised His disciples that the Holy Spirit would come to dwell within them. This promise is recorded in several passages of the Gospels, emphasizing the importance of the Holy Spirit in the life of the believer.

- John 14:16-17: "And I will pray the Father, and He will give you another Helper, that He may abide with you forever—the Spirit of truth, whom the world cannot receive, because it neither sees Him nor knows Him; but you know Him, for He dwells with you and will be in you."

Jesus refers to the Holy Spirit as "another Helper" (Greek: παράκλητος, parakletos - Strong's G3875), indicating that the Spirit would continue Jesus' work in the lives of His followers. The promise that the Spirit would "be in you" highlights the personal and intimate nature of the Spirit's indwelling.

- John 16:7: "Nevertheless I tell you the truth. It is to your advantage that I go away; for if I do not go away, the Helper will not come to you; but if I depart, I will send Him to you."

Jesus explains that His departure (through the crucifixion, resurrection, and ascension) is necessary for the Holy Spirit to come. The arrival of the Holy Spirit marks the beginning of a new era in which believers would experience the indwelling presence of God in a way that was not possible before.

20.2.2 The Fulfillment of the Promise: The Day of Pentecost

The promise of the Holy Spirit's indwelling was fulfilled on the day of Pentecost, as recorded in the book of Acts. This event marked the beginning of the Church and the indwelling of the Holy Spirit in every believer.

- Acts 2:1-4: "When the Day of Pentecost had fully come, they were all with one accord in one place. And suddenly there came a sound from heaven, as of a rushing mighty wind, and it filled the whole house where they were sitting. Then there appeared to them divided tongues, as of fire, and one sat upon each of them. And they were all filled with the Holy Spirit and began to speak with other tongues, as the Spirit gave them utterance."

The filling of the Holy Spirit at Pentecost is the fulfillment of Jesus' promise. The indwelling of the Holy Spirit is not a temporary experience but a permanent reality for every believer, signifying their union with Christ and their participation in the divine nature.

20.2.3 The Ongoing Reality of the Holy Spirit's Indwelling

The indwelling of the Holy Spirit is not limited to the first disciples; it is the ongoing reality for all who place their faith in Jesus Christ. The apostle Paul emphasizes this truth in his letters, underscoring the transformative power of the Holy Spirit in the believer's life.

- Romans 8:9-11: "But you are not in the flesh but in the Spirit, if indeed the Spirit of God dwells in you. Now if anyone does not have the Spirit of Christ, he is not His. And if Christ is in you, the body is dead because of sin, but the Spirit is life because of righteousness. But if the Spirit of Him who raised Jesus from the dead dwells in you, He who raised Christ from the dead will also give life to your mortal bodies through His Spirit who dwells in you."

Paul's words make it clear that the indwelling of the Holy Spirit is the defining mark of a true believer. The Spirit's presence within the believer not only brings life but also unites the believer with Christ, enabling them to participate in His divine nature.

20.3 Theological Significance of the Holy Spirit's Indwelling

The indwelling of the Holy Spirit is rich with theological significance, particularly in how it unites believers with the divine nature of Christ. This union is not merely a metaphor but a profound spiritual reality that transforms the believer from the inside out.

20.3.1 Participation in the Divine Nature

One of the most significant aspects of the Holy Spirit's indwelling is that it enables believers to participate in the divine nature of Christ. This participation is a key theme in the New Testament and is particularly emphasized by the apostle Peter.

- 2 Peter 1:3-4: "As His divine power has given to us all things that pertain to life and godliness, through the knowledge of Him who called us by glory and virtue, by which have been given to us exceedingly great and precious promises, that through these you may be partakers of the divine nature, having escaped the corruption that is in the world through lust."

The term "partakers" (Greek: κοινωνοί, koinonoi - Strong's G2844) means "sharers" or "partners." Through the indwelling of the Holy Spirit, believers are brought into a deep union with Christ, sharing in His divine life and holiness. This participation in the divine nature is not about becoming gods but about being transformed into the image of Christ, who is the perfect image of God.

20.3.2 Union with Christ

The indwelling of the Holy Spirit is the means by which believers are united with Christ. This union is described in various ways throughout the New Testament, often using the metaphor of the body.

- 1 Corinthians 6:17: "But he who is joined to the Lord is one spirit with Him."

- Ephesians 1:13-14: "In Him you also trusted, after you heard the word of truth, the gospel of your salvation; in whom also, having believed, you were sealed with the Holy Spirit of promise, who is the guarantee of our inheritance until the redemption of the purchased possession, to the praise of His glory."

The Holy Spirit acts as the seal and guarantee of the believer's union with Christ. This union is both spiritual and sacramental, as it is through the Holy Spirit that believers are incorporated into the body of Christ and made one with Him.

20.3.3 Transformation into Christ's Image

The indwelling of the Holy Spirit not only unites believers with Christ but also transforms them into His image. This process of transformation, known as sanctification, is the work of the Holy Spirit in making believers more like Christ in character and conduct.

- 2 Corinthians 3:18: "But we all, with unveiled face, beholding as in a mirror the glory of the Lord, are being transformed into the same image from glory to glory, just as by the Spirit of the Lord."

- Romans 8:29: "For whom He foreknew, He also predestined to be conformed to the image of His Son, that He might be the firstborn among many brethren."

The Holy Spirit's work of sanctification is a gradual but powerful process by which believers are conformed to the image of Christ. This transformation is a direct result of the believer's union with Christ through the Spirit, as the divine nature of Christ is imparted to them.

20.3.4 The Spirit as the Source of Spiritual Life

The indwelling Holy Spirit is the source of spiritual life for the believer. This life is not merely a continuation of natural existence but a new kind of life—eternal life, which is the life of God Himself.

- John 6:63: "It is the Spirit who gives life; the flesh profits nothing. The words that I speak to you are spirit, and they are life."

- Galatians 2:20: "I have been crucified with Christ; it is no longer I who live, but Christ lives in me; and the life which I now live in the flesh I live by faith in the Son of God, who loved me and gave Himself for me."

The life that believers now live is the life of Christ, made possible by the indwelling of the Holy Spirit. This spiritual life is characterized by a relationship with God, holiness, and the power to overcome sin.

20.4 Practical Implications of the Holy Spirit's Indwelling

The indwelling of the Holy Spirit has profound practical implications for the life of the believer. It affects every aspect of Christian living, from personal holiness to relationships within the Church and the world.

20.4.1 Empowerment for Holy Living

The indwelling Holy Spirit empowers believers to live holy lives that reflect the character of Christ. This empowerment is not about human effort but about yielding to the Spirit's work within.

- Galatians 5:16-17: "I say then:

Walk in the Spirit, and you shall not fulfill the lust of the flesh. For the flesh lusts against the Spirit, and the Spirit against the flesh; and these are contrary to one another, so that you do not do the things that you wish."

- Ephesians 5:18: "And do not be drunk with wine, in which is dissipation; but be filled with the Spirit."

Walking in the Spirit means living under the Spirit's guidance and control, allowing Him to produce the fruit of the Spirit in our lives (Galatians 5:22-23). This leads to a life that is characterized by love, joy, peace, and all the virtues that reflect the divine nature of Christ.

20.4.2 Unity and Fellowship in the Body of Christ

The Holy Spirit's indwelling also brings believers into unity with one another as members of the body of Christ. This unity is not uniformity but a profound spiritual connection that transcends differences and fosters genuine fellowship.

- 1 Corinthians 12:12-13: "For as the body is one and has many members, but all the members of that one body, being many, are one body, so also is Christ. For by one Spirit we were all baptized into one body—whether Jews or Greeks, whether slaves or free—and have all been made to drink into one Spirit."

- Ephesians 4:3-4: "Endeavoring to keep the unity of the Spirit in the bond of peace. There is one body and one Spirit, just as you were called in one hope of your calling."

The Holy Spirit is the source of the Church's unity, and this unity is expressed in the love, service, and mutual edification that believers share. The Spirit's indwelling enables believers to live in harmony, overcoming divisions and working together for the common good.

20.4.3 Witness and Mission

The indwelling Holy Spirit empowers believers for witness and mission, enabling them to share the Gospel and live out their faith in the world. This empowerment is seen in the boldness and effectiveness of the early Church and continues to be a vital aspect of Christian mission today.

- Acts 1:8: "But you shall receive power when the Holy Spirit has come upon you; and you shall be witnesses to Me in Jerusalem, and in all Judea and Samaria, and to the end of the earth."

- 1 Peter 3:15: "But sanctify the Lord God in your hearts, and always be ready to give a defense to everyone who asks you a reason for the hope that is in you, with meekness and fear."

The Holy Spirit equips believers with the gifts and boldness needed to proclaim the Gospel and to live as witnesses of Christ in a world that often opposes Him. This witness is not just verbal but is also demonstrated in a life that reflects the love and truth of Christ.

20.4.4 Assurance and Comfort

Finally, the indwelling Holy Spirit provides believers with assurance of their salvation and comfort in times of trial. The Spirit's presence within us is a constant reminder of God's love and faithfulness.

- Romans 8:16: "The Spirit Himself bears witness with our spirit that we are children of God."

- John 14:26: "But the Helper, the Holy Spirit, whom the Father will send in My name, He will teach you all things, and bring to your remembrance all things that I said to you."

The Holy Spirit assures believers of their identity as children of God and comforts them with the knowledge of God's presence and promises. This assurance is vital for maintaining faith and hope in the midst of life's challenges.

20.5 Conclusion

The indwelling of the Holy Spirit is one of the most transformative and empowering aspects of the Christian life. Through the Spirit's indwelling, believers are united with the divine nature of Christ, participating in His life, holiness, and mission. This union is both a present reality and a foretaste of the eternal life that awaits believers in the fullness of God's kingdom.

As believers, we are called to live in the power of the Holy Spirit, allowing Him to transform us into the image of Christ and to equip us for the work of the Gospel. The Spirit's indwelling is a gift of God's grace, a sign of His love, and a guarantee of our future inheritance in Christ.

In a world that is often marked by division, strife, and uncertainty, the indwelling of the Holy Spirit offers believers a source of unity, strength, and hope. By embracing this gift and walking in the Spirit, we can live lives that reflect the divine nature of Christ and bear witness to His saving power in a world in need of redemption.

Living in the Power of the Holy Spirit

The Practical Outworking of Jesus' Divinity in the Life of a Christian

21.1 Introduction

The divinity of Jesus Christ is not merely a theological concept but a reality that has profound implications for the everyday life of a Christian. Through the power of the Holy Spirit, believers are enabled to live out the divine nature of Christ in their daily lives. This chapter explores how living in the power of the Holy Spirit manifests the practical outworking of Jesus' divinity, transforming the believer's character, guiding their actions, and empowering them for service in the Kingdom of God.

21.2 The Holy Spirit as the Source of Spiritual Life

The Holy Spirit is the source of the believer's spiritual life, making the life of Christ real and active within them. This spiritual life is characterized by a deep and personal relationship with God, marked by growth in holiness and the manifestation of the fruit of the Spirit.

21.2.1 New Birth and Spiritual Renewal

The Christian life begins with the new birth, a spiritual transformation that is brought about by the Holy Spirit. This new birth is essential for entering into the Kingdom of God and experiencing the life of Christ.

- John 3:5-6: "Jesus answered, 'Most assuredly, I say to you, unless one is born of water and the Spirit, he cannot enter the kingdom of God. That which is born of the flesh is flesh, and that which is born of the Spirit is spirit.'"

The new birth, or regeneration, is the work of the Holy Spirit in bringing a person from spiritual death to spiritual life. This transformation is the foundation for living in the power of the Holy Spirit, as it marks the beginning of a new life in Christ.

21.2.2 The Indwelling Presence of Christ

Through the Holy Spirit, Jesus Christ dwells within the believer, making His divine life and power accessible to them. This indwelling presence is the key to living a life that reflects the character and mission of Christ.

- Galatians 2:20: "I have been crucified with Christ; it is no longer I who live, but Christ lives in me; and the life which I now live in the flesh I live by faith in the Son of God, who loved me and gave Himself for me."

The indwelling of Christ through the Holy Spirit empowers believers to live out their faith with the assurance that they are never alone. The presence of Christ within them provides the strength and guidance needed to navigate the challenges of life while remaining faithful to God's calling.

21.2.3 The Fruit of the Spirit

The practical outworking of Jesus' divinity in the life of a Christian is most clearly seen in the fruit of the Spirit. These virtues are the evidence of the Holy Spirit's work in transforming the believer's character to reflect the nature of Christ.

- Galatians 5:22-23: "But the fruit of the Spirit is love, joy, peace, longsuffering, kindness, goodness, faithfulness, gentleness, self-control. Against such there is no law."

The fruit of the Spirit are not merely ethical standards but are the natural result of the Holy Spirit's presence in the believer's life. As believers walk in the Spirit, these qualities become increasingly evident, demonstrating the practical impact of Jesus' divinity on their daily lives.

21.3 Walking in the Spirit: Daily Dependence on God

Living in the power of the Holy Spirit requires a daily dependence on God, characterized by a lifestyle of walking in the Spirit. This walk is an intentional choice to follow the leading of the Holy Spirit rather than relying on human effort or worldly wisdom.

21.3.1 Being Led by the Spirit

Walking in the Spirit means being led by the Spirit in all aspects of life. This involves seeking God's guidance in decision-making, relationships, and personal growth, trusting that the Holy Spirit will direct the believer according to God's will.

- Romans 8:14: "For as many as are led by the Spirit of God, these are sons of God."

Being led by the Spirit is a mark of spiritual maturity and sonship. It requires sensitivity to the Spirit's promptings and a willingness to submit to His guidance, even when it challenges personal desires or societal norms.

21.3.2 Overcoming the Flesh

One of the primary challenges of living in the power of the Holy Spirit is overcoming the desires of the flesh—those sinful inclinations that oppose the work of the Spirit. Walking in the Spirit involves a daily battle against the flesh, with the assurance that victory is possible through the Spirit's power.

- Galatians 5:16-17: "I say then: Walk in the Spirit, and you shall not fulfill the lust of the flesh. For the flesh lusts against the Spirit, and the Spirit against the flesh; and these are contrary to one another, so that you do not do the things that you wish."

The Holy Spirit provides the strength needed to resist temptation and to live a life that is pleasing to God. By walking in the Spirit, believers are able to overcome the power of sin and experience the freedom that comes from living in accordance with God's will.

21.3.3 The Discipline of Prayer and the Word

A life lived in the power of the Holy Spirit is rooted in the disciplines of prayer and engagement with the Word of God. These spiritual practices are essential for maintaining a close relationship with God and for discerning the leading of the Holy Spirit.

- Ephesians 6:18: "Praying always with all prayer and supplication in the Spirit, being watchful to this end with all perseverance and supplication for all the saints."

- Colossians 3:16: "Let the word of Christ dwell in you richly in all wisdom, teaching and admonishing one another in psalms and hymns and spiritual songs, singing with grace in your hearts to the Lord."

Prayer in the Spirit is a vital means of communication with God, allowing the believer to align their heart and mind with His purposes. Similarly, allowing the Word of Christ to dwell richly within the believer equips them with the knowledge and wisdom needed to live a Spirit-filled life.

21.4 Empowerment for Mission and Service

Living in the power of the Holy Spirit is not just about personal transformation; it also involves being empowered for mission and service. The Holy Spirit equips believers with spiritual gifts and the boldness needed to fulfill the Great Commission and to serve others in love.

21.4.1 The Gifts of the Spirit

The Holy Spirit bestows various spiritual gifts upon believers, enabling them to contribute to the building up of the Church and the advancement of God's Kingdom. These gifts are diverse, reflecting the different ways in which the Holy Spirit works through individuals to accomplish God's purposes.

- 1 Corinthians 12:4-7: "There are diversities of gifts, but the same Spirit. There are differences of ministries, but the same Lord. And there are diversities of activities, but it is the same God who works all in all. But the manifestation of the Spirit is given to each one for the profit of all."

Spiritual gifts are not given for personal gain but for the common good, allowing the Church to function as the body of Christ. By exercising their gifts in the power of the

Holy Spirit, believers participate in the divine mission of Christ, bringing His presence and power to the world.

21.4.2 Boldness in Witness

The power of the Holy Spirit is evident in the boldness with which believers proclaim the Gospel. This boldness is not a natural courage but a supernatural empowerment that comes from the Spirit, enabling believers to speak the truth of Christ with conviction and love.

- Acts 4:31: "And when they had prayed, the place where they were assembled together was shaken; and they were all filled with the Holy Spirit, and they spoke the word of God with boldness."

Boldness in witness is a hallmark of a life lived in the power of the Holy Spirit. It reflects the believer's confidence in the truth of the Gospel and their commitment to making Christ known, regardless of opposition or persecution.

21.4.3 Serving Others in Love

The Holy Spirit also empowers believers to serve others in love, reflecting the self-giving nature of Christ. This service is not motivated by duty or obligation but by the love of Christ, which the Holy Spirit pours into the hearts of believers.

- Galatians 5:13-14: "For you, brethren, have been called to liberty; only do not use liberty as an opportunity for the flesh, but through love serve one another. For all the law is fulfilled in one word, even in this: 'You shall love your neighbor as yourself.'"

Serving others in the power of the Holy Spirit is a practical outworking of Jesus' divinity in the life of a Christian. It involves meeting the needs of others, whether physical, emotional, or spiritual, and doing so with the love and compassion of Christ.

21.5 The Assurance and Comfort of the Holy Spirit

Living in the power of the Holy Spirit also brings assurance and comfort to believers. The Holy Spirit's presence provides the assurance of salvation, the comfort of God's love, and the peace that surpasses all understanding.

21.5.1 Assurance of Salvation

The Holy Spirit bears witness to the believer's spirit, providing assurance of their identity as a child of God and their eternal security in Christ.

- Romans 8:16: "The Spirit Himself bears witness with our spirit that we are children of God."

- Ephesians 1:13-14: "In Him you also trusted, after you heard the word of truth, the gospel of your salvation; in whom also, having believed, you were sealed with the Holy Spirit of promise, who is the guarantee of our inheritance until the redemption of the purchased possession, to the praise of His glory."

This assurance is not based on feelings or circumstances but on the unchanging promises of God and the inner witness of the Holy Spirit. It gives believers confidence in their salvation and hope for the future.

21.5.2 Comfort in Times of Trial

The Holy Spirit is also the Comforter, providing peace and strength in times of trial and difficulty. The comfort of the Holy Spirit is a reminder of God's presence and His faithfulness, even in the midst of suffering.

- John 14:26-27: "But the Helper, the Holy Spirit, whom the Father will send in My name, He will teach you all things, and bring to your remembrance all things that I said to you. Peace I leave with you, My peace I give to you; not as the world gives do I give to you. Let not your heart be troubled, neither let it be afraid."

The peace that the Holy Spirit provides is a reflection of the peace of Christ, which transcends earthly troubles and provides a sense of calm and trust in God's sovereign care.

21.6 Conclusion

Living in the power of the Holy Spirit is the practical outworking of Jesus' divinity in the life of a Christian. It involves a daily dependence on the Holy Spirit for guidance, strength, and transformation. Through the Holy Spirit, believers are united with Christ, empowered for mission and service, and equipped to live lives that reflect the character of Christ.

The Holy Spirit's presence in the believer's life is not a passive experience but an active partnership in the work of God's Kingdom. It is through the power of the Holy Spirit that believers can overcome the challenges of life, grow in holiness, and make a meaningful impact in the world for Christ.

As Christians live in the power of the Holy Spirit, they bear witness to the reality of Jesus' divinity and His ongoing work in the world. This life in the Spirit is not only a testimony to others but also a source of joy, peace, and assurance for the believer, as they experience the fullness of life that Jesus came to give.

CHAPTER 08

THEOLOGICAL REFLECTIONS ON THE DIVINITY OF CHRIST

Early Church Fathers on Jesus' Divinity: Exploring the Views of Key Theologians like Augustine and Athanasius

22.1 Introduction

The doctrine of the divinity of Jesus Christ is central to Christian theology, forming the foundation of the faith and shaping the Church's understanding of salvation, the Trinity, and the nature of God. Throughout the history of the Church, this doctrine has been defended, articulated, and developed by many theologians, particularly during the early centuries of Christianity. Among the most influential of these early Church Fathers are Augustine of Hippo and Athanasius of Alexandria. Their contributions to the understanding of Jesus' divinity have left an indelible mark on Christian theology, influencing the development of key doctrines and creeds that continue to define orthodox Christian belief. This chapter explores the views of Augustine and Athanasius on the divinity of Christ, highlighting their theological contributions and the enduring significance of their teachings.

22.2 Athanasius of Alexandria: Defender of the Divinity of Christ

Athanasius of Alexandria (c. 296-373 AD) is one of the most prominent figures in early Christian theology, particularly known for his defense of the doctrine of Christ's divinity against the heresy of Arianism. His steadfast commitment to the truth of Christ's divine nature earned him the title "Athanasius contra mundum" ("Athanasius against the world").

22.2.1 The Challenge of Arianism

Arianism, named after its proponent Arius, was a theological doctrine that denied the full divinity of Jesus Christ. Arius taught that Jesus was a created being, distinct from and subordinate to God the Father, and therefore not fully divine. This heresy posed a significant threat to the Church's understanding of the Trinity and the nature of salvation.

- Arius' View: Arius argued that there was a time when the Son did not exist, asserting that the Son was the first and greatest of God's creations but was not co-eternal with the Father. He famously declared, "There was a time when He was not," implying that the Son was not divine in the same way as the Father.

Athanasius recognized that if Arius' views were accepted, it would undermine the entire foundation of Christian theology. Without the full divinity of Christ, the doctrine of the Trinity would collapse, and the efficacy of Christ's redemptive work would be called into question.

22.2.2 Athanasius' Defense of Christ's Divinity

In response to Arianism, Athanasius devoted his life to defending the orthodox Christian understanding of Christ's divinity. His most significant work, On the Incarnation of the Word, presents a compelling argument for the full divinity of Christ and the necessity of the Incarnation for human salvation.

- On the Incarnation: Athanasius argues that only God Himself could save humanity from sin and death. If Jesus were merely a creature, He would not have the power to redeem humanity. Therefore, the Word (Logos), who is co-eternal and consubstantial with the Father, took on human flesh to accomplish the work of salvation.

- Key Quote: "For He was made man that we might be made God" (Athanasius, On the Incarnation). This statement encapsulates Athanasius' belief in the transformative power of the Incarnation, where the divine Word assumes human nature to restore humanity to communion with God.

Athanasius also played a crucial role in the formulation of the Nicene Creed at the First Council of Nicaea in 325 AD, where the Church affirmed that the Son is "of the same substance" (homoousios) as the Father. This creed became the standard of orthodox Christian belief, rejecting Arianism and solidifying the doctrine of Christ's divinity.

22.2.3 The Legacy of Athanasius

Athanasius' unwavering defense of Christ's divinity ensured that the doctrine would remain a cornerstone of Christian theology. His contributions laid the groundwork for later theological developments and have continued to influence Christian thought for centuries.

- Athanasius and the Trinity: Athanasius' articulation of the relationship between the Father and the Son was foundational for the development of the doctrine of the Trinity. By affirming that the Son is co-eternal and consubstantial with the Father, Athanasius helped to clarify the understanding of the Trinity as one God in three persons.

- Athanasius and the Incarnation: Athanasius' emphasis on the Incarnation as the means of salvation highlighted the importance of Christ's divinity in the redemptive work. His teaching that the divine Word became flesh to restore humanity to God has remained a central theme in Christian soteriology.

22.3 Augustine of Hippo: The Theologian of Grace and the Trinity

Augustine of Hippo (354-430 AD) is one of the most influential theologians in the history of Christianity. His writings on the nature of God, the Trinity, grace, and salvation have shaped Western Christian thought for centuries. Augustine's reflections on the divinity of Christ are deeply connected to his understanding of the Trinity and the nature of grace.

22.3.1 Augustine's Understanding of the Trinity

Augustine's most comprehensive treatment of the Trinity is found in his work De Trinitate (On the Trinity), where he explores the relationship between the Father, Son, and Holy Spirit. Augustine sought to explain the mystery of the Trinity in a way that was both faithful to Scripture and philosophically rigorous.

- The Eternal Generation of the Son: Augustine emphasized the doctrine of the eternal generation of the Son, meaning that the Son is eternally begotten of the Father, not created or made. This begetting does not imply any form of inferiority or temporality but rather affirms the Son's co-eternity and consubstantiality with the Father.

- Key Quote: "The Son is not less than the Father, for both together are one God" (Augustine, De Trinitate). Augustine insisted that the Son, though begotten, is fully divine and shares the same essence as the Father, thus maintaining the unity and equality of the Trinity.

- The Holy Spirit as the Bond of Love: Augustine described the Holy Spirit as the bond of love between the Father and the Son. This conception highlights the relational nature of the Trinity, where the three persons are united in an eternal exchange of love. The Holy Spirit's role as the bond of love underscores the inseparability of the divine persons and the unity of the Godhead.

22.3.2 Augustine on the Divinity of Christ

For Augustine, the divinity of Christ was central to his understanding of salvation and grace. He taught that only a divine Savior could accomplish the work of redemption, and that this work was made possible through the Incarnation of the Word.

- The Incarnation and Redemption: Augustine saw the Incarnation as the ultimate act of divine love, where God became man to redeem humanity from sin. The Word (Logos), who is fully God, took on human nature to bridge the gap between God and fallen humanity.

- Key Quote: "He who is truly the Son of God, the Word of God, who was in the beginning with God, through whom all things were made, was made flesh and dwelt among us" (Augustine, Confessions). Augustine's understanding of the Incarnation emphasizes the continuity between the divine and human natures of Christ, affirming that the same Word who created the world is the one who redeems it.

- Christ as the Mediator: Augustine emphasized the role of Christ as the mediator between God and humanity. As both fully divine and fully human, Christ is uniquely qualified to reconcile humanity to God, making Him the only means of salvation.

- Key Quote: "There is one mediator between God and men, the man Christ Jesus, who gave Himself as a ransom for all" (1 Timothy 2:5-6, quoted by Augustine). Augustine's understanding of Christ as the mediator highlights the necessity of His divinity in effecting reconciliation and atonement.

22.3.3 Augustine on Grace and the Divinity of Christ

Augustine's doctrine of grace is deeply intertwined with his understanding of Christ's divinity. He taught that salvation is a gift of God's grace, made possible only through the divine work of Christ.

- Grace as Unmerited Favor: Augustine argued that human beings, because of their fallen nature, are incapable of achieving salvation through their own efforts. Salvation is entirely dependent on God's grace, which is given freely through Christ.

- Key Quote: "By grace you have been saved through faith, and this is not your own doing; it is the gift of God" (Ephesians 2:8, quoted by Augustine). Augustine's emphasis on grace underscores the necessity of Christ's divinity, as only God can grant the grace that leads to salvation.

- The Role of the Holy Spirit: Augustine also emphasized the role of the Holy Spirit in applying the grace of Christ to the believer. The Holy Spirit, who proceeds from the Father and the Son, works within the believer to bring about transformation and sanctification.

- Key Quote: "The Holy Spirit is the gift of God, who brings us into the life of grace and makes us partakers of the divine nature" (Augustine, On the Spirit and the Letter). Augustine's understanding of the Holy Spirit's role in salvation highlights the Trinitarian nature of grace, where the work of salvation is accomplished by the Father, Son, and Holy Spirit.

22.4 The Enduring Influence of Augustine and Athanasius

The theological contributions of Augustine and Athanasius have had a lasting impact on Christian theology, particularly in the areas of Christology, Trinitarian doctrine, and soteriology. Their teachings continue to inform and shape the Church's understanding of the divinity of Christ and the nature of salvation.

22.4.1 The Nicene Creed and Christian Orthodoxy

The work of Athanasius was instrumental in the formulation of the Nicene Creed, which remains a foundational statement of Christian orthodoxy. The creed's affirmation of the consubstantiality of the Son with the Father ("of one substance with the Father") is a direct result of Athanasius' defense of Christ's divinity.

- The Nicene Creed: "We believe in one Lord Jesus Christ, the only-begotten Son of God, begotten of the Father before all worlds, Light of Light, very God of very God, begotten, not made, being of one substance with the Father; by whom all things were made."

This creed, which was later expanded at the Council of Constantinople in 381 AD, remains a central confession of faith for Christians worldwide and is recited in many Christian liturgies.

22.4.2 Augustine's Influence on Western Theology

Augustine's influence on Western Christianity is unparalleled. His writings have shaped the development of Christian thought in areas such as original sin, predestination, the sacraments, and the relationship between faith and reason.

- Augustine's Legacy: Augustine's emphasis on the necessity of grace, the centrality of Christ's divinity, and the relational nature of the Trinity has had a profound impact on both Catholic and Protestant theology. His works, such as The Confessions, The City of God, and On the Trinity, continue to be studied and revered by theologians and laypeople alike.

22.4.3 The Ongoing Relevance of Patristic Theology

The teachings of the early Church Fathers, including Augustine and Athanasius, remain relevant for contemporary theology. Their reflections on the divinity of Christ provide a foundation for understanding the Christian faith and for engaging with modern theological challenges.

- Patristic Theology Today: In an age where the divinity of Christ is sometimes questioned or misunderstood, the writings of the early Church Fathers serve as a vital resource for defending and articulating the doctrine of

Christ's divinity. Their works remind the Church of the importance of maintaining the integrity of the Christian faith as it was handed down by the apostles and defended by the early theologians.

22.5 Conclusion

The divinity of Jesus Christ is a central tenet of Christian theology, one that has been carefully articulated and defended by the early Church Fathers. Athanasius of Alexandria and Augustine of Hippo are two of the most significant figures in this regard, each contributing to the development of the doctrine of Christ's divinity in profound ways.

Athanasius' defense of Christ's divinity against Arianism ensured that the Church would maintain an orthodox understanding of the Trinity and the Incarnation. His teachings on the necessity of the divine Word becoming flesh continue to influence Christian thought on the nature of salvation and the person of Christ.

Augustine's reflections on the Trinity, grace, and the Incarnation have shaped the course of Western Christian theology. His emphasis on the relational nature of the Trinity and the centrality of Christ's divinity in the work of salvation remains foundational for understanding the Christian faith.

The teachings of these early Church Fathers provide a rich theological heritage that continues to inform and inspire Christians today. Their insights into the mystery of Christ's divinity challenge believers to deepen their understanding of the faith and to live in the reality of the Incarnation, where God became man to redeem and restore His creation.

The Nicene Creed

How the Early Church Formalized the Belief in Jesus' Divinity

23.1 Introduction

The doctrine of the divinity of Jesus Christ is the cornerstone of Christian theology. However, this belief was not always formally articulated or universally agreed upon in the early Church. As Christianity spread throughout the Roman Empire, various interpretations of Christ's nature began to emerge, leading to significant theological disputes. These disputes threatened to divide the Church and undermine the core tenets of the Christian faith. In response, the early Church sought to formalize its beliefs through the creation of creeds—authoritative statements of faith that clarified essential doctrines. The most significant of these is the Nicene Creed, formulated at the First Council of Nicaea in 325 AD. This chapter explores how the early Church came to formalize the belief in Jesus' divinity through the Nicene Creed, examining the historical context, key theological debates, and the enduring impact of this foundational document.

23.2 The Historical Context of the Nicene Creed

The creation of the Nicene Creed was driven by the need to address the theological controversies that were threatening the unity of the early Church. The most prominent of these controversies was Arianism, a doctrine that challenged the full divinity of Jesus Christ.

23.2.1 The Rise of Arianism

Arianism, named after its proponent Arius, a presbyter from Alexandria, emerged in the early 4th century as a significant theological challenge. Arius taught that Jesus, the Son of God, was not co-eternal with the Father but was a created being, distinct from and subordinate to the Father.

- Arius' Doctrine: Arius argued that "there was a time when the Son was not," implying that the Son was a creature who came into existence by the will of the Father. According to Arius, the Son was the first and greatest of all created beings but was not of the same substance (Greek: homoousios) as the Father.

This teaching directly contradicted the traditional understanding of Jesus' divinity, which held that the Son was co-eternal and consubstantial with the Father. Arianism quickly gained a significant following, leading to deep divisions within the Church.

23.2.2 The Council of Nicaea

In response to the growing controversy, Emperor Constantine, who had recently converted to Christianity, convened the First Council of Nicaea in 325 AD. The council was held in the city of Nicaea (modern-day İznik, Turkey) and brought together bishops from across the Roman Empire to address the Arian heresy and to restore unity to the Church.

- Constantine's Role: Constantine's decision to convene the council was motivated by his desire to maintain peace and stability in the empire, which he believed could be threatened by religious divisions. Although Constantine did not take a direct role in the theological debates, his presence and support gave the council significant political and ecclesiastical authority.

- The Purpose of the Council: The primary goal of the Council of Nicaea was to resolve the theological dispute over the nature of Christ and to establish a clear and authoritative statement of faith that could be accepted by all Christians. The council aimed to preserve the apostolic faith and to safeguard the Church from doctrinal error.

23.3 The Theological Debates at Nicaea

The theological debates at the Council of Nicaea were intense and deeply significant, as they centered on the very nature of Jesus Christ and His relationship to God the Father. The key issue was whether Jesus was fully divine and of the same essence as the Father or whether He was a created being, as Arius claimed.

23.3.1 The Key Participants

The debates at Nicaea involved several key figures who played crucial roles in shaping the outcome of the council and the formulation of the Nicene Creed.

- Arius: As the proponent of the Arian doctrine, Arius argued that the Son was created by the Father and therefore could not be of the same essence as the Father. He maintained that the Son was subordinate to the Father and was not co-eternal with Him.

- Athanasius: A deacon at the time and later the Bishop of Alexandria, Athanasius was one of the most ardent defenders of the orthodox position that the Son was fully divine and consubstantial with the Father. He argued that only if the Son was truly God could He offer salvation to humanity.

- Eusebius of Nicomedia: A supporter of Arius, Eusebius of Nicomedia advocated for a more conciliatory approach, suggesting a compromise that would acknowledge the Son's divinity but avoid the term homoousios ("of the same substance"). His proposal, however, was ultimately rejected.

- Alexander of Alexandria: The Bishop of Alexandria and the mentor of Athanasius, Alexander strongly opposed Arianism and supported the use of the term homoousios to describe the relationship between the Father and the Son.

23.3.2 The Debate Over Homoousios

The central theological debate at Nicaea revolved around the term homoousios, which means "of the same substance" or "consubstantial." This term was proposed to affirm that the Son was not a created being but was of the same divine essence as the Father.

- Arian Position: The Arians rejected the term homoousios because it implied that the Son was equal to the Father and shared the same divine nature. They preferred the term homoiousios, meaning "of similar substance," which would allow for a distinction between the Father and the Son.

- Orthodox Position: The supporters of the orthodox position, including Athanasius, argued that homoousios was necessary to preserve the full divinity of the Son. They contended that if the Son were not of the same essence as the Father, He could not be truly God, and the doctrine of the Trinity would be compromised.

The debate over homoousios was not merely a semantic issue but a fundamental question about the nature of God and the possibility of salvation. The council ultimately rejected the Arian position and affirmed the use of homoousios in the creed, thereby declaring that the Son is of the same substance as the Father and fully divine.

23.3.3 The Formulation of the Nicene Creed

The outcome of the Council of Nicaea was the formulation of the Nicene Creed, a definitive statement of Christian faith that articulated the Church's belief in the full divinity of Jesus Christ.

- The Nicene Creed: "We believe in one God, the Father Almighty, Maker of heaven and earth, and of all things visible and invisible. And in one Lord Jesus Christ, the only-begotten Son of God, begotten of the Father before all worlds; Light of Light, very God of very God; begotten, not made, being of one substance (homoousios) with the Father, by whom all things were made."

The Nicene Creed explicitly affirms that Jesus Christ is "very God of very God" and "of one substance with the Father." By including these statements, the creed rejects Arianism and establishes the orthodox belief that the Son is fully divine and co-eternal with the Father.

- Anathemas Against Arianism: The creed also includes anathemas, or condemnations, against those who hold to the Arian position, declaring that anyone who denies that the Son is of the same substance as the Father is outside the bounds of orthodox Christian belief.

23.4 The Impact of the Nicene Creed on Christian Theology

The Nicene Creed had a profound and lasting impact on Christian theology, serving as a foundational statement of faith for the Church. It provided a clear and authoritative articulation of the doctrine of Christ's divinity and became a touchstone for subsequent theological developments.

23.4.1 The Establishment of Orthodox Christology

The Nicene Creed established the orthodox understanding of Christology, affirming the full divinity of Jesus Christ and His consubstantiality with the Father. This Christological foundation became essential for the development of other key doctrines, including the Trinity and the nature of salvation.

- The Trinity: The affirmation of the Son's divinity in the Nicene Creed paved the way for a fuller articulation of the doctrine of the Trinity. The creed implicitly upholds the belief in one God in three persons—Father, Son, and Holy Spirit—each of whom shares the same divine essence.

- Salvation: By affirming the divinity of Christ, the Nicene Creed also underpins the Christian understanding of salvation. Only a Savior who is fully divine can reconcile humanity to God and offer redemption from sin and death.

23.4.2 The Role of the Nicene Creed in Later Councils

The Nicene Creed served as a basis for further theological reflection and was expanded at subsequent councils, particularly the First Council of Constantinople in 381 AD. The expanded creed, often referred to as the Niceno-Constantinopolitan Creed, reaffirmed the doctrines established at Nicaea and included additional statements about the Holy Spirit.

- Council of Constantinople: The First Council of Constantinople reaffirmed the Nicene Creed and further clarified the doctrine of the Holy Spirit, affirming that the Spirit is also consubstantial with the Father and the Son. This council addressed the heresy of Macedonianism, which denied the divinity of the Holy Spirit.

- The Niceno-Constantinopolitan Creed: The expanded creed included the phrase, "And in the Holy Spirit, the Lord and Giver of life, who proceeds from the

Father, who with the Father and the Son together is worshiped and glorified." This statement further solidified the doctrine of the Trinity and the full divinity of each person of the Godhead.

23.4.3 The Enduring Significance of the Nicene Creed

The Nicene Creed has endured as a central confession of Christian faith, recited in liturgies across various Christian traditions, including Roman Catholic, Eastern Orthodox, Anglican, and Protestant churches. Its significance lies in its ability to articulate the core beliefs of Christianity in a way that is both concise and theologically profound.

- Ecumenical Importance: The Nicene Creed is recognized as an ecumenical statement of faith, meaning it is accepted by Christians across denominational lines. It serves as a unifying document that expresses the shared beliefs of the global Christian community.

- Doctrinal Stability: The Nicene Creed has provided doctrinal stability for the Church, serving as a benchmark for orthodoxy. Throughout history, various heresies and theological disputes have arisen, but the Nicene Creed has remained a touchstone for determining what constitutes authentic Christian belief.

23.5 Conclusion

The Nicene Creed is one of the most important documents in the history of Christianity. It represents the early Church's effort to formalize and defend the belief in

Jesus' divinity in the face of significant theological challenges. Through the work of the Council of Nicaea, the Church affirmed that Jesus Christ is fully divine, co-eternal, and consubstantial with the Father, laying the foundation for the doctrine of the Trinity and the Christian understanding of salvation.

The legacy of the Nicene Creed continues to shape Christian theology and worship to this day. It provides a clear and authoritative statement of faith that has withstood the test of time, serving as a guide for Christians in understanding the nature of God and the person of Jesus Christ. The creed's emphasis on the divinity of Christ is not only a doctrinal affirmation but also a declaration of the Church's faith in the transformative power of the Incarnation, where God became man to redeem and restore His creation.

As Christians recite the Nicene Creed in their liturgies and personal devotions, they join in a centuries-old tradition of proclaiming the truth of Christ's divinity and the mystery of the Trinity—a truth that remains at the heart of the Christian faith.

Contemporary Views and Challenges

Addressing Modern Debates and Affirming Traditional Christian Doctrine

24.1 Introduction

The divinity of Jesus Christ, a cornerstone of traditional Christian doctrine, continues to be a subject of theological reflection and debate in contemporary times. While the early Church Fathers and councils, such as the Council of Nicaea, established a clear orthodox understanding of Christ's divinity, modern theological perspectives and cultural shifts have introduced new challenges to this foundational belief. In this chapter, we will explore the contemporary views and challenges related to the doctrine of Christ's divinity, addressing both the debates that arise within the Christian community and the external pressures from secular thought. By affirming traditional Christian doctrine in light of these challenges, we seek to maintain the integrity of the faith handed down through the centuries.

24.2 Modern Theological Debates on Christ's Divinity

In contemporary theology, several debates have emerged regarding the nature of Christ's divinity. These debates often reflect broader questions about the interpretation of Scripture, the relevance of traditional doctrine in a modern context, and the relationship between faith and reason.

24.2.1 The Quest for the Historical Jesus

One of the significant movements in contemporary theology is the "Quest for the Historical Jesus," which seeks to understand Jesus primarily as a historical figure, often at the expense of traditional doctrinal affirmations about His divinity. This movement has its roots in 19th-century biblical criticism and has evolved through various phases, with scholars attempting to distinguish the "Jesus of history" from the "Christ of faith."

- Key Issues: The quest often involves a critical examination of the Gospel accounts, with some scholars arguing that the divinity of Christ was a later theological development rather than a belief held by the earliest Christians. These scholars may downplay or reinterpret the miraculous elements of the Gospels and question the reliability of certain biblical narratives.

- Response: Traditional Christian doctrine affirms that the divinity of Christ is not a later invention but is rooted in the earliest Christian witness, as seen in the New Testament writings and the creeds of the early Church. The Gospels, while containing historical elements, also present theological truths that cannot be fully understood if Jesus' divinity is denied. The quest for the historical Jesus must be balanced with a recognition of the theological significance of the Incarnation and the resurrection.

24.2.2 Christology from Below vs. Christology from Above

Another contemporary debate involves the distinction between "Christology from below" and "Christology from above." Christology from below begins with the human Jesus and seeks to understand His divinity in light of His earthly life, while Christology from above starts with the pre-existent divine Logos and emphasizes the divine nature of Christ.

- Christology from Below: This approach often focuses on Jesus' humanity, His moral teachings, and His role as a social reformer. It may emphasize Jesus as a model for human behavior and downplay His divine attributes.

- Christology from Above: This approach affirms the pre-existence of Christ as the divine Word and focuses on the significance of the Incarnation as God becoming man. It emphasizes the divinity of Christ and His role in the cosmic plan of salvation.

- Response: Traditional Christian doctrine holds that both aspects of Christ's nature—His humanity and divinity— must be fully affirmed. The Chalcedonian Definition (451 AD) declares that Christ is "one person in two natures, fully God and fully man." Any Christology that neglects either aspect risks distorting the true identity of Jesus as presented in the Scriptures and the creeds.

24.2.3 The Influence of Religious Pluralism

In an increasingly pluralistic world, the exclusive claims of Christianity, particularly the divinity of Christ, are often challenged. Religious pluralism promotes the idea that all religions are equally valid paths to God, which can lead to a relativistic approach to Christ's divinity.

- Key Issues: Religious pluralism may argue that Jesus is one of many divine figures or that His divinity is a culturally specific interpretation rather than a universal truth. This view can undermine the uniqueness of Christ and the Christian claim that Jesus is the only way to God (John 14:6).

- Response: Traditional Christian doctrine affirms that Jesus Christ is the unique and definitive revelation of God, fully divine and the only mediator between God and humanity (1 Timothy 2:5). While respecting the religious beliefs of others, Christianity maintains the conviction that the divinity of Christ is an essential and non-negotiable truth of the faith.

24.3 Secular Challenges to the Divinity of Christ

Beyond theological debates within the Church, the doctrine of Christ's divinity faces challenges from secular thought, particularly in the realms of science, philosophy, and contemporary culture.

24.3.1 The Challenge of Scientism

Scientism is the belief that empirical science is the only valid way to acquire knowledge, leading to the rejection of metaphysical or theological claims. This worldview can challenge the divinity of Christ by denying the possibility of miracles, the supernatural, or any reality beyond the material world.

- Key Issues: Scientism may view the doctrine of Christ's divinity as unscientific or irrational, arguing that beliefs about Jesus' divine nature are based on myth rather than evidence. This perspective can lead to a dismissal of religious faith as irrelevant or outdated.

- Response: Traditional Christian doctrine asserts that faith and reason are not in conflict but are complementary ways of knowing. The divinity of Christ is a truth that transcends empirical verification, rooted in the revelation of God through Scripture, tradition, and the witness of the Church. While science can explain the natural world, it cannot fully account for the mysteries of faith, including the Incarnation and the resurrection.

24.3.2 The Influence of Postmodernism

Postmodernism, with its emphasis on relativism and the rejection of absolute truths, presents a challenge to the traditional understanding of Christ's divinity. In a postmodern context, the idea of an absolute, universal truth is often viewed with skepticism, and religious beliefs are seen as subjective or culturally constructed.

- Key Issues: Postmodernism may lead to the view that the divinity of Christ is just one interpretation among many, shaped by historical and cultural contexts rather than reflecting an objective reality. This can result in a relativistic approach to theology, where all beliefs are considered equally valid.

- Response: Traditional Christian doctrine affirms that the divinity of Christ is not merely a cultural construct but a revealed truth with universal significance. The Church's proclamation of Christ as "very God of very God" (Nicene Creed) is based on the belief that God has revealed Himself definitively in Jesus Christ, whose divinity is not subject to human reinterpretation but is a truth that transcends all cultures and contexts.

24.3.3 The Challenge of Secular Humanism

Secular humanism emphasizes human reason, ethics, and justice while rejecting religious beliefs as unnecessary for moral living. This worldview can challenge the divinity of Christ by promoting a purely humanistic understanding of Jesus as a moral teacher or social reformer rather than as the divine Son of God.

- Key Issues: Secular humanism may admire Jesus as a figure of ethical wisdom and compassion but reject any claims about His divinity or the necessity of faith in Him for salvation. This approach can reduce Christianity to a set of moral principles without acknowledging its foundational theological claims.

- Response: Traditional Christian doctrine insists that while Jesus is indeed a moral teacher, His teachings cannot be separated from His identity as the divine Son of God. The ethical teachings of Jesus are rooted in His divine authority, and His role as Savior is central to the Christian understanding of human dignity, justice, and redemption. Without affirming Christ's divinity, the full meaning and transformative power of His message are lost.

24.4 Affirming Traditional Christian Doctrine in Contemporary Contexts

In the face of these modern debates and secular challenges, it is essential for the Church to reaffirm and articulate the traditional doctrine of Christ's divinity. This involves engaging with contemporary culture and thought while remaining rooted in the historic faith of the Church.

24.4.1 The Role of Apologetics

Apologetics, the reasoned defense of the faith, plays a crucial role in affirming the divinity of Christ in contemporary contexts. By addressing the intellectual challenges posed by modern thought, apologetics helps to demonstrate the coherence and credibility of Christian doctrine.

- Engaging with Science and Philosophy: Apologists can engage with scientific and philosophical questions, showing that belief in Christ's divinity is rational and compatible with a robust understanding of the world. This may involve addressing common misconceptions about the relationship between faith and reason and presenting a case for the existence of God and the truth of the Incarnation.

- Addressing Cultural Relativism: Apologetics can also respond to the relativism of postmodernism by articulating the uniqueness and universality of Christ's divinity. This involves demonstrating that the Christian faith offers not just one option among many but the true and ultimate revelation of God in history.

24.4.2 The Importance of Creeds and Confessions

In a time of doctrinal uncertainty, the historic creeds and confessions of the Church, such as the Nicene Creed, serve as vital tools for maintaining orthodoxy and providing a clear articulation of the faith.

- Reciting and Teaching the Creeds: The regular recitation of the creeds in Christian worship serves as a reminder of the Church's shared beliefs and its commitment to the truth of Christ's divinity. Teaching the creeds to new generations of believers helps to ground them in the historic faith and equips them to withstand modern challenges.

- Confessional Integrity: Maintaining confessional integrity involves upholding the creeds and confessions as authoritative standards of doctrine. This means that theological innovations or reinterpretations must be evaluated in light of the established teachings of the Church, ensuring that the core truths of the faith are preserved.

24.4.3 The Witness of the Church in the World

The Church's witness to the divinity of Christ is not only a matter of doctrinal affirmation but also of living out the implications of this belief in the world. The Church is called to embody the truth of Christ's divinity through its worship, service, and proclamation.

- Worshiping Christ as Lord: Worship is the primary expression of the Church's belief in Christ's divinity. By gathering to worship Jesus as Lord and God, the Church proclaims His divine authority and sovereignty over all creation.

- Proclaiming the Gospel: The Church's mission involves proclaiming the Gospel of Jesus Christ, emphasizing His divinity as central to the message of salvation. Evangelism and mission efforts must be rooted in the conviction that

Jesus is the way, the truth, and the life, and that faith in Him is necessary for eternal life.

- Serving in the Name of Christ: The Church's service to the world—whether through acts of charity, social justice, or pastoral care—is an outworking of its belief in Christ's divinity. By serving others in the name of Jesus, the Church reflects His love and lordship, demonstrating that He is not just a moral teacher but the divine Savior who transforms lives.

24.5 Conclusion

The doctrine of Christ's divinity remains a central and essential aspect of the Christian faith, one that has been affirmed and defended throughout the history of the Church. In contemporary times, this doctrine faces new challenges, both from within the Church and from the broader culture. However, by engaging thoughtfully with these challenges and reaffirming the traditional teachings of the faith, the Church can continue to uphold the truth of Christ's divinity and its implications for the world.

As Christians navigate the complexities of modern theology and secular thought, they are called to remain faithful to the historic faith of the Church, as articulated in the creeds and confessions. By doing so, they bear witness to the reality of the Incarnation, where God became man in the person of Jesus Christ to redeem and restore His creation. In this truth lies the hope and power of the Christian Gospel, a message that remains as relevant and transformative today as it was in the earliest days of the Church.

CHAPTER 09

THE WORK OF THE HOLY SPIRIT IN THE CHURCH TODAY

Continuing the Ministry of Jesus: How the Holy Spirit Empowers the Church to Continue Jesus' Work

25.1 Introduction

The ministry of Jesus Christ on earth was characterized by teaching, healing, proclaiming the Kingdom of God, and demonstrating God's love and power. However, Jesus' earthly ministry did not end with His ascension. Instead, He promised to send the Holy Spirit, who would empower His disciples to continue His work. The Holy Spirit's role in the Church today is to equip and empower believers to carry on the ministry of Jesus, ensuring that His mission continues to advance in the world. This chapter explores how the Holy

Spirit empowers the Church to continue Jesus' work, examining the biblical foundations, the manifestation of the Spirit's power in the life of the Church, and the practical outworking of this empowerment in the mission and ministry of believers.

25.2 The Promise of the Holy Spirit

Before His ascension, Jesus assured His disciples that they would not be left alone to carry on His work. He promised to send the Holy Spirit, who would empower them for the mission ahead.

25.2.1 The Holy Spirit as the Advocate and Helper

In the Gospel of John, Jesus refers to the Holy Spirit as the Advocate or Helper (Greek: Parakletos), who would come to guide, teach, and empower His followers.

- John 14:16-17: "And I will pray the Father, and He will give you another Helper, that He may abide with you forever—the Spirit of truth, whom the world cannot receive, because it neither sees Him nor knows Him; but you know Him, for He dwells with you and will be in you."

- John 16:7: "Nevertheless I tell you the truth. It is to your advantage that I go away; for if I do not go away, the Helper will not come to you; but if I depart, I will send Him to you."

The term Parakletos conveys the idea of someone who comes alongside to offer support, guidance, and advocacy. Jesus' promise of the Holy Spirit as the Parakletos assured the disciples that they would not be left to fend for themselves. The Spirit would be their guide, teacher, and source of strength as they continued Jesus' work.

25.2.2 The Empowerment for Witness

In the book of Acts, Jesus explicitly connects the coming of the Holy Spirit with the empowerment of His disciples to be His witnesses in the world.

- Acts 1:8: "But you shall receive power when the Holy Spirit has come upon you; and you shall be witnesses to Me in Jerusalem, and in all Judea and Samaria, and to the end of the earth."

The Greek word for "power" (dynamis) indicates a dynamic, miraculous power that enables the disciples to carry out their mission effectively. This empowerment by the Holy Spirit is not just for personal spiritual growth but for the purpose of extending the reach of the Gospel to all nations.

25.3 The Manifestation of the Holy Spirit's Power in the Church

The presence and power of the Holy Spirit in the Church are evident in various ways, all of which contribute to continuing the ministry of Jesus. These manifestations include the gifts of the Spirit, the fruit of the Spirit, and the guidance of the Spirit.

25.3.1 The Gifts of the Spirit

The Holy Spirit bestows a variety of spiritual gifts upon believers, equipping them to serve the Church and advance the Kingdom of God. These gifts are given for the common good and are essential for the Church's mission.

- 1 Corinthians 12:4-7: "There are diversities of gifts, but the same Spirit. There are differences of ministries, but the same Lord. And there are diversities of activities, but it is the same God who works all in all. But the manifestation of the Spirit is given to each one for the profit of all."

The gifts of the Spirit include wisdom, knowledge, faith, healing, miracles, prophecy, discerning of spirits, tongues, and interpretation of tongues (1 Corinthians 12:8-10). Each gift plays a unique role in building up the Church and enabling believers to continue the work of Jesus.

- Romans 12:6-8: "Having then gifts differing according to the grace that is given to us, let us use them: if prophecy, let us prophesy in proportion to our faith; or ministry, let us use it in our ministering; he who teaches, in teaching; he who exhorts, in exhortation; he who gives, with liberality; he who leads, with diligence; he who shows mercy, with cheerfulness."

These gifts empower believers to preach the Gospel, teach the Word of God, heal the sick, serve others, and lead the Church in fulfilling its mission.

25.3.2 The Fruit of the Spirit

In addition to the gifts of the Spirit, the Holy Spirit also produces the fruit of the Spirit in the lives of believers. These qualities reflect the character of Christ and are essential for effective ministry.

- Galatians 5:22-23: "But the fruit of the Spirit is love, joy, peace, longsuffering, kindness, goodness, faithfulness, gentleness, self-control. Against such there is no law."

The fruit of the Spirit is the evidence of the Spirit's work in transforming the believer's character. As believers grow in the fruit of the Spirit, they become more like Jesus, and their lives bear witness to the transforming power of the Gospel.

- Ephesians 5:9: "For the fruit of the Spirit is in all goodness, righteousness, and truth."

The cultivation of the fruit of the Spirit is essential for the Church's witness in the world. It ensures that the message of the Gospel is communicated not only through words but also through the lives of those who proclaim it.

25.3.3 The Guidance of the Holy Spirit

The Holy Spirit provides guidance to believers, helping them to discern God's will and to make decisions that align with His purposes. This guidance is crucial for the Church's mission, as it ensures that believers are led by the Spirit rather than by human wisdom.

- Romans 8:14: "For as many as are led by the Spirit of God, these are sons of God."

- John 16:13: "However, when He, the Spirit of truth, has come, He will guide you into all truth; for He will not speak on His own authority, but whatever He hears He will speak; and He will tell you things to come."

The Holy Spirit's guidance is manifested in various ways, including through Scripture, prayer, prophetic insights, and the counsel of other believers. By following the Spirit's leading, the Church can remain faithful to its mission and avoid the pitfalls of human error.

25.4 The Practical Outworking of the Holy Spirit's Empowerment in the Church's Ministry

The empowerment of the Holy Spirit is not merely a theological concept but has practical implications for the Church's ministry. This empowerment enables the Church to carry on the work of Jesus in several key areas.

25.4.1 Evangelism and Mission

One of the primary ways the Holy Spirit empowers the Church to continue Jesus' work is through evangelism and mission. The Holy Spirit emboldens believers to proclaim the Gospel and equips them to reach people from all walks of life.

- Acts 4:31: "And when they had prayed, the place where they were assembled together was shaken; and they were all filled with the Holy Spirit, and they spoke the word of God with boldness."

The Spirit's power in evangelism is evident in the boldness with which believers witness to the truth of the Gospel. This boldness is not natural but is a result of the Holy Spirit's work in the hearts of believers, enabling them to overcome fear and opposition.

- Acts 13:2-4: "As they ministered to the Lord and fasted, the Holy Spirit said, 'Now separate to Me Barnabas and Saul for the work to which I have called them.' Then, having fasted and prayed, and laid hands on them, they sent them away. So, being sent out by the Holy Spirit, they went down to Seleucia, and from there they sailed to Cyprus."

The Holy Spirit also directs the Church's mission, calling and sending individuals to specific places and tasks. The success of missionary endeavors depends on the guidance and empowerment of the Holy Spirit, who opens doors, prepares hearts, and brings about the growth of the Kingdom.

25.4.2 Healing and Deliverance

The ministry of Jesus was marked by healing and deliverance, and the Holy Spirit empowers the Church to continue this aspect of His work. Through the Spirit, believers can pray for the sick, cast out demons, and bring freedom to those who are oppressed.

- Mark 16:17-18: "And these signs will follow those who believe: In My name they will cast out demons; they will speak with new tongues; they will take up serpents; and if they drink anything deadly, it will by no means hurt them; they will lay hands on the sick, and they will recover."

The signs that accompany the preaching of the Gospel, including healing and deliverance, testify to the power of Jesus' name and the presence of the Kingdom of God. The Holy Spirit works through these signs to confirm the message of the Gospel and to demonstrate God's love and compassion.

- James 5:14-15: "Is anyone among you sick? Let him call for the elders of the church, and let them pray over him, anointing him with oil in the name of the Lord. And the prayer of faith will save the sick, and the Lord will raise him up."

The ministry of healing in the Church today is a continuation of Jesus' healing work, empowered by the Holy Spirit. It is a tangible expression of God's care for His people and a powerful witness to the reality of the Gospel.

25.4.3 Discipleship and Teaching

The Holy Spirit also empowers the Church to continue Jesus' work through discipleship and teaching. The Spirit guides believers into all truth and enables them to grow in their understanding of God's Word.

- John 14:26: "But the Helper, the Holy Spirit, whom the Father will send in My name, He will teach you all things, and bring to your remembrance all things that I said to you."

The Holy Spirit's role as the Teacher ensures that the Church remains rooted in the truth of the Gospel. Through the Spirit, believers are equipped to teach others, to make disciples, and to pass on the faith to future generations.

- 2 Timothy 2:2: "And the things that you have heard from me among many witnesses, commit these to faithful men who will be able to teach others also."

The work of discipleship is essential to the Church's mission, and it is through the empowerment of the Holy Spirit that this work is carried out effectively. The Spirit not only imparts knowledge but also transforms hearts, enabling believers to live out the teachings of Jesus in their daily lives.

25.4.4 Social Justice and Compassion

The Holy Spirit empowers the Church to continue Jesus' work of bringing justice, compassion, and care to the marginalized and oppressed. The Spirit moves believers to act in love and to advocate for the poor, the vulnerable, and the disenfranchised.

- Luke 4:18-19: "The Spirit of the Lord is upon Me, because He has anointed Me to preach the gospel to the poor; He has sent Me to heal the brokenhearted, to proclaim liberty to the captives and recovery of sight to the blind, to set at liberty those who are oppressed; to proclaim the acceptable year of the Lord."

The ministry of social justice and compassion is a direct continuation of Jesus' mission, as outlined in His proclamation in the synagogue at Nazareth. The Holy Spirit empowers believers to address the social and economic injustices of their time, to care for the needy, and to work for the transformation of society.

- Micah 6:8: "He has shown you, O man, what is good; and what does the Lord require of you but to do justly, to love mercy, and to walk humbly with your God?"

The Church's commitment to justice and mercy is a reflection of the character of Christ and is sustained by the empowerment of the Holy Spirit. This work involves not only acts of charity but also advocacy, systemic change, and the pursuit of peace and reconciliation.

25.5 Conclusion

The Holy Spirit plays a crucial role in empowering the Church to continue the ministry of Jesus. Through the Spirit, believers are equipped to preach the Gospel, heal the sick, make disciples, and work for justice in the world. The power of the Holy Spirit is not limited to the early Church but is available to all believers today, enabling them to carry out the mission of Jesus with boldness, compassion, and effectiveness.

As the Church continues to rely on the Holy Spirit, it can faithfully carry on the work of Jesus, making His presence known in the world and advancing the Kingdom of God. The Spirit's empowerment is not just a privilege but a responsibility, calling believers to live out their faith in ways that reflect the love, power, and truth of Christ. Through the Holy Spirit, the Church is not only a witness to what Jesus has done but also an active participant in what He continues to do, bringing hope, healing, and transformation to a world in need.

Gifts of the Spirit and Jesus' Authority

The Connection Between Spiritual Gifts and Jesus' Divine Mission

26.1 Introduction

The gifts of the Holy Spirit are vital tools given to believers to equip them for the mission of the Church, which is to continue the work of Jesus Christ in the world. These spiritual gifts are not just abilities or talents; they are manifestations of the Holy Spirit's power and presence in the life of the Church. The gifts of the Spirit are intrinsically connected to Jesus' divine mission, as they enable the Church to exercise His authority and extend His ministry. In this chapter, we will explore the connection between spiritual gifts and Jesus' authority, examining how these gifts function within the Church to fulfill the divine mission of Christ and how they reflect and extend Jesus' own authority and power.

26.2 Understanding the Gifts of the Spirit

The gifts of the Spirit are diverse and are given to believers to serve the common good and to build up the body of Christ. They are distributed by the Holy Spirit according to His will and are intended to manifest the presence of God within the Church and in the world.

26.2.1 Biblical Foundations of Spiritual Gifts

The New Testament provides several lists of spiritual gifts, emphasizing their variety and their role in the life of the Church.

- 1 Corinthians 12:4-11: "There are diversities of gifts, but the same Spirit. There are differences of ministries, but the same Lord. And there are diversities of activities, but it is the same God who works all in all. But the manifestation of the Spirit is given to each one for the profit of all: for to one is given the word of wisdom through the Spirit, to another the word of knowledge through the same Spirit, to another faith by the same Spirit, to another gifts of healings by the same Spirit, to another the working of miracles, to another prophecy, to another discerning of spirits, to another different kinds of tongues, to another the interpretation of tongues. But one and the same Spirit works all these things, distributing to each one individually as He wills."

- Romans 12:6-8: "Having then gifts differing according to the grace that is given to us, let us use them: if prophecy, let us prophesy in proportion to our faith; or ministry, let us use it in our ministering; he who teaches, in teaching; he who exhorts, in exhortation; he who gives, with liberality; he who leads, with diligence; he who shows mercy, with cheerfulness."

- Ephesians 4:11-13: "And He Himself gave some to be apostles, some prophets, some evangelists, and some pastors and teachers, for the equipping of the saints for the work of ministry, for the edifying of the body of Christ, till we all come to the unity of the faith and of the knowledge of the Son of God, to a perfect man, to the measure of the stature of the fullness of Christ."

These passages highlight the diversity of spiritual gifts and their purpose in the Church. Each gift serves a unique function, contributing to the overall health and mission of the Church.

26.2.2 The Purpose of Spiritual Gifts

The primary purpose of spiritual gifts is to build up the body of Christ and to enable the Church to fulfill its mission. Spiritual gifts are not given for personal gain or status but for the benefit of others and the glorification of God.

- 1 Corinthians 14:12: "Even so you, since you are zealous for spiritual gifts, let it be for the edification of the church that you seek to excel."

- Ephesians 4:12-13: "For the equipping of the saints for the work of ministry, for the edifying of the body of Christ, till we all come to the unity of the faith and of the knowledge of the Son of God, to a perfect man, to the measure of the stature of the fullness of Christ."

Spiritual gifts are essential for the Church's ministry because they empower believers to serve in ways that extend beyond their natural abilities. They enable the Church to carry out the work of Jesus, continuing His mission of proclaiming the Kingdom of God, healing the sick, and bringing justice and peace to the world.

26.3 The Connection Between Spiritual Gifts and Jesus' Authority

The authority of Jesus Christ is the foundation for the operation of spiritual gifts within the Church. These gifts are manifestations of Jesus' ongoing presence and power, exercised through the Holy Spirit, who continues the work of Jesus in and through the Church.

26.3.1 Jesus' Authority in the Gospels

Throughout the Gospels, Jesus is portrayed as one who possesses divine authority. This authority is evident in His teaching, His miracles, His ability to forgive sins, and His command over the forces of nature and the spiritual realm.

- Matthew 7:28-29: "And so it was, when Jesus had ended these sayings, that the people were astonished at His teaching, for He taught them as one having authority, and not as the scribes."

- Mark 2:10-12: "But that you may know that the Son of Man has power on earth to forgive sins—He said to the paralytic, 'I say to you, arise, take up your bed, and go to your house.' Immediately he arose, took up the bed, and went out in the presence of them all, so that all were amazed and glorified God, saying, 'We never saw anything like this!'"

- Luke 8:24-25: "And they came to Him and awoke Him, saying, 'Master, Master, we are perishing!' Then He arose and rebuked the wind and the raging of the water. And they ceased, and there was a calm. But He said to them, 'Where is your faith?' And they were afraid, and marveled, saying to one another, 'Who can this be? For He commands even the winds and water, and they obey Him!'"

Jesus' authority is not merely a human authority but a divine authority, rooted in His identity as the Son of God. This authority is passed on to His disciples, who are commissioned to continue His work.

26.3.2 The Great Commission and the Delegation of Authority

Before His ascension, Jesus commissioned His disciples to continue His work, delegating His authority to them through the power of the Holy Spirit.

- Matthew 28:18-20: "And Jesus came and spoke to them, saying, 'All authority has been given to Me in heaven and on earth. Go therefore and make disciples of all the nations, baptizing them in the name of the Father and of the

Son and of the Holy Spirit, teaching them to observe all things that I have commanded you; and lo, I am with you always, even to the end of the age.'"

- Acts 1:8: "But you shall receive power when the Holy Spirit has come upon you; and you shall be witnesses to Me in Jerusalem, and in all Judea and Samaria, and to the end of the earth."

The Great Commission is a mandate for the Church to continue the ministry of Jesus, empowered by the Holy Spirit. The authority that Jesus exercised during His earthly ministry is now exercised by the Church through the operation of spiritual gifts. These gifts are the means by which the Church carries out the mission of Christ, extending His authority and presence in the world.

26.3.3 Spiritual Gifts as Expressions of Jesus' Authority

The spiritual gifts given to the Church are expressions of Jesus' authority, exercised through the Holy Spirit. Each gift reflects an aspect of Jesus' ministry and extends His work in the world.

- Healing and Miracles: The gifts of healing and miracles are direct continuations of Jesus' healing ministry. Just as Jesus healed the sick and performed miracles to demonstrate the coming of the Kingdom of God, the Church is empowered to do the same through the Holy Spirit.

- Matthew 10:7-8: "And as you go, preach, saying, 'The kingdom of heaven is at hand.' Heal the sick, cleanse the lepers, raise the dead, cast out demons. Freely you have received, freely give."

- Prophecy and Wisdom: The gift of prophecy continues Jesus' role as the Prophet who speaks God's truth to the people. Similarly, the word of wisdom reflects Jesus' divine wisdom, guiding the Church in decisions and revealing God's will.

- Luke 4:18-19: "The Spirit of the Lord is upon Me, because He has anointed Me to preach the gospel to the poor; He has sent Me to heal the brokenhearted, to proclaim liberty to the captives and recovery of sight to the blind, to set at liberty those who are oppressed; to proclaim the acceptable year of the Lord."

- Teaching and Shepherding: The gifts of teaching and shepherding (pastoral leadership) reflect Jesus' ministry as the Good Shepherd and Teacher. These gifts are essential for guiding the Church in truth and nurturing the spiritual growth of believers.

- John 10:14: "I am the good shepherd; and I know My sheep, and am known by My own."

Each spiritual gift, whether it is a word of knowledge, faith, helps, or administration, contributes to the continuation of Jesus' ministry. Through these gifts, the Church exercises the authority of Jesus, advancing His mission and manifesting His presence in the world.

26.4 The Impact of Spiritual Gifts on the Church's Mission

The spiritual gifts given to the Church are not only for internal edification but also for the broader mission of advancing the Kingdom of God. The effective use of these gifts is crucial for the Church to fulfill its calling.

26.4.1 Building Up the Body of Christ

One of the primary purposes of spiritual gifts is to build up the body of Christ, ensuring that the Church is healthy, united, and equipped for its mission.

- Ephesians 4:11-13: "And He Himself gave some to be apostles, some prophets, some evangelists, and some pastors and teachers, for the equipping of the saints for the work of ministry, for the edifying of the body of Christ, till we all come to the unity of the faith and of the knowledge of the Son of God, to a perfect man, to the measure of the stature of the fullness of Christ."

When the Church operates in the gifts of the Spirit, it grows in maturity and unity, reflecting the fullness of Christ.

This growth is not only for the benefit of believers but also for the effectiveness of the Church's witness in the world.

26.4.2 Empowering the Church for Evangelism and Mission

The gifts of the Spirit empower the Church to engage in evangelism and mission, reaching out to the world with the message of the Gospel. The signs and wonders that accompany the proclamation of the Gospel are testimonies to the truth of Jesus' authority and His power to save.

- Mark 16:17-18, 20: "And these signs will follow those who believe: In My name they will cast out demons; they will speak with new tongues; they will take up serpents; and if they drink anything deadly, it will by no means hurt them; they will lay hands on the sick, and they will recover... And they went out and preached everywhere, the Lord working with them and confirming the word through the accompanying signs. Amen."

The operation of spiritual gifts in evangelism serves as a demonstration of God's power and draws people to faith in Christ. Through these gifts, the Church is able to engage in effective mission, reaching the lost and proclaiming the Kingdom of God.

26.4.3 Demonstrating the Kingdom of God

The gifts of the Spirit are also a foretaste of the Kingdom of God, demonstrating the reality of God's reign in the present age. Through the exercise of spiritual gifts, the Church provides glimpses of the fullness of the Kingdom, where God's will is done on earth as it is in heaven.

- 1 Corinthians 4:20: "For the kingdom of God is not in word but in power."

The power of the Kingdom is made manifest through the gifts of the Spirit, as the Church exercises Jesus' authority in healing the sick, casting out demons, and proclaiming the Gospel. These acts are signs of the in-breaking Kingdom, pointing to the ultimate fulfillment of God's promises.

26.5 Conclusion

The connection between spiritual gifts and Jesus' divine mission is essential for understanding the role of the Holy Spirit in the life of the Church. The gifts of the Spirit are not merely tools for individual edification but are integral to the Church's mission of continuing the work of Jesus in the world. These gifts are expressions of Jesus' authority, delegated to the Church through the Holy Spirit, and they enable believers to carry out the mission of the Kingdom with power and effectiveness.

As the Church operates in the gifts of the Spirit, it continues the ministry of Jesus, demonstrating His authority, advancing His mission, and manifesting His presence in the world. The effective use of spiritual gifts is a testament to the ongoing work of Christ through His Church, as believers are empowered by the Holy Spirit to proclaim the Gospel, heal the sick, build up the body of Christ, and extend the reign of God's Kingdom on earth. Through these gifts, the Church not only honors the legacy of Jesus but also participates in His divine mission, bringing hope, healing, and salvation to a world in need.

The Holy Spirit and Christian Unity

How the Spirit Unites Believers in Recognizing and Worshiping Jesus as Lord

27.1 Introduction

Christian unity is a central theme in the New Testament and a vital aspect of the Church's witness in the world. This unity, however, is not based merely on shared beliefs or practices but is rooted in the work of the Holy Spirit. The Holy Spirit plays a crucial role in uniting believers across diverse cultures, traditions, and denominations by enabling them to recognize and worship Jesus as Lord. This chapter explores how the Holy Spirit fosters Christian unity, focusing on the Spirit's role in bringing believers together in faith, worship, and mission.

27.2 The Foundation of Christian Unity in the Holy Spirit

The unity of the Church is fundamentally a work of the Holy Spirit. It is the Spirit who creates and sustains the bond of unity among believers, drawing them together into one body under the lordship of Jesus Christ.

27.2.1 The Spirit's Role in Baptism and Incorporation into the Body of Christ

Christian unity begins with the believer's incorporation into the body of Christ through baptism, a work of the Holy Spirit. In baptism, believers are united with Christ in His death and resurrection and are made members of His body, the Church.

- 1 Corinthians 12:13: "For by one Spirit we were all baptized into one body—whether Jews or Greeks, whether slaves or free—and have all been made to drink into one Spirit."

The act of baptism is not just a symbolic ritual but a spiritual reality in which the Holy Spirit unites believers with Christ and with one another. This incorporation into the body of Christ transcends all social, cultural, and ethnic distinctions, creating a new community of faith that is united by the Spirit.

27.2.2 The Unity of the Spirit in the Bond of Peace

The Holy Spirit not only initiates Christian unity but also sustains it through the bond of peace. The unity that the Spirit creates is marked by peace, mutual love, and the shared confession of Jesus as Lord.

- Ephesians 4:3-6: "Endeavoring to keep the unity of the Spirit in the bond of peace. There is one body and one Spirit, just as you were called in one hope of your calling; one Lord, one faith, one baptism; one God and Father of all, who is above all, and through all, and in you all."

The unity of the Spirit is a gift that believers are called to maintain. This unity is rooted in the shared experience of the Holy Spirit, who brings believers into a relationship with the one Lord, one faith, and one baptism. The bond of peace that the Spirit creates is essential for the Church's witness and mission, as it reflects the peace of Christ and the reconciliation He has brought to the world.

27.3 The Spirit's Work in Recognizing Jesus as Lord

A central aspect of Christian unity is the shared recognition and confession of Jesus as Lord. The Holy Spirit plays a crucial role in revealing the lordship of Jesus to believers and enabling them to respond in faith and worship.

27.3.1 The Spirit's Revelation of Jesus' Lordship

The Holy Spirit is the one who reveals Jesus to believers, opening their eyes to His true identity as the Son of

God and the Savior of the world. Without the work of the Spirit, no one can truly recognize Jesus as Lord.

- 1 Corinthians 12:3: "Therefore I make known to you that no one speaking by the Spirit of God calls Jesus accursed, and no one can say that Jesus is Lord except by the Holy Spirit."

This passage underscores the fact that the confession of Jesus as Lord is not merely an intellectual assent but a revelation given by the Holy Spirit. It is the Spirit who illuminates the hearts and minds of believers, enabling them to see Jesus for who He truly is and to acknowledge His lordship in their lives.

27.3.2 Unity in Worshiping Jesus as Lord

The recognition of Jesus as Lord leads to the worship of Him as God. The Holy Spirit unites believers in worship, drawing them together to glorify Jesus and to offer their lives in service to Him.

- Philippians 2:9-11: "Therefore God also has highly exalted Him and given Him the name which is above every name, that at the name of Jesus every knee should bow, of those in heaven, and of those on earth, and of those under the earth, and that every tongue should confess that Jesus Christ is Lord, to the glory of God the Father."

The worship of Jesus as Lord is a unifying act for the Church. Regardless of cultural or denominational differences, all Christians are united in their worship of Jesus. The Holy Spirit empowers this worship, leading believers to bow before Jesus and to confess Him as Lord.

27.3.3 The Role of the Spirit in Corporate Worship

The Holy Spirit's work in uniting believers is especially evident in corporate worship, where the body of Christ gathers to express their shared faith and devotion to Jesus. In worship, the Spirit moves among believers, enabling them to worship in spirit and truth.

- John 4:23-24: "But the hour is coming, and now is, when the true worshipers will worship the Father in spirit and truth; for the Father is seeking such to worship Him. God is Spirit, and those who worship Him must worship in spirit and truth."

The Spirit's presence in worship creates an atmosphere of unity, where believers, regardless of their backgrounds, can come together to worship the Lord. The Spirit leads the congregation in worship, guiding the prayers, songs, and praises that are offered to God. This shared experience of worship deepens the unity of the Church and strengthens the bonds of fellowship among believers.

27.4 The Spirit and Unity in Diversity

One of the remarkable aspects of Christian unity is that it is a unity in diversity. The Holy Spirit brings together people from different cultures, languages, and traditions, uniting them in Christ while celebrating their diversity.

27.4.1 The Pentecost Event: A Model of Unity in Diversity

The event of Pentecost provides a powerful example of how the Holy Spirit creates unity in diversity. On the day of Pentecost, the Holy Spirit was poured out on the disciples, and they began to speak in various languages, enabling people from different regions to hear the Gospel in their own tongue.

- Acts 2:4-6: "And they were all filled with the Holy Spirit and began to speak with other tongues, as the Spirit gave them utterance. And there were dwelling in Jerusalem Jews, devout men, from every nation under heaven. And when this sound occurred, the multitude came together, and were confused, because everyone heard them speak in his own language."

Pentecost demonstrates that the Holy Spirit values cultural and linguistic diversity, using it as a means to proclaim the Gospel. The unity created by the Spirit does not erase differences but brings people together across those differences, uniting them in the shared recognition of Jesus as Lord.

27.4.2 The Gifts of the Spirit and Unity in Diversity

The diversity of spiritual gifts within the Church is another way the Holy Spirit creates unity in diversity. The Spirit distributes a variety of gifts to different members of the Church, all of which are essential for the functioning of the body of Christ.

- 1 Corinthians 12:4-6: "There are diversities of gifts, but the same Spirit. There are differences of ministries, but the same Lord. And there are diversities of activities, but it is the same God who works all in all."

The different gifts given by the Spirit contribute to the overall unity of the Church, as each member uses their gift for the common good. This diversity of gifts reflects the creativity and wisdom of the Holy Spirit, who brings together different talents and abilities to build up the body of Christ.

27.4.3 Overcoming Division and Fostering Reconciliation

The Holy Spirit also plays a crucial role in overcoming division within the Church and fostering reconciliation. Where there are conflicts or divisions, the Spirit works to bring healing and restore unity.

- Ephesians 2:14-18: "For He Himself is our peace, who has made both one, and has broken down the middle wall of separation... and that He might reconcile them both to

God in one body through the cross, thereby putting to death the enmity. And He came and preached peace to you who were afar off and to those who were near. For through Him we both have access by one Spirit to the Father."

The Spirit's work of reconciliation is essential for maintaining unity within the Church. Through the Spirit, believers are empowered to forgive one another, to seek peace, and to work together in harmony, reflecting the unity that exists in the Godhead.

27.5 The Mission of the Church and the Unity of the Spirit

Christian unity, fostered by the Holy Spirit, is not an end in itself but serves the greater purpose of the Church's mission in the world. A united Church is a powerful witness to the reality of Jesus' lordship and the transformative power of the Gospel.

27.5.1 Unity as a Witness to the World

Jesus prayed for the unity of His followers, recognizing that their unity would be a powerful testimony to the world of His divine mission.

- John 17:20-21: "I do not pray for these alone, but also for those who will believe in Me through their word; that they all may be one, as You, Father, are in Me, and I in You;

that they also may be one in Us, that the world may believe that You sent Me."

The unity of believers is a reflection of the unity between the Father and the Son, and it serves as a witness to the world that Jesus is the Son of God. The Holy Spirit is the one who brings about this unity, making it possible for the Church to fulfill its mission of proclaiming the Gospel.

27.5.2 The Spirit's Empowerment for Mission

The unity created by the Holy Spirit also empowers the Church for mission. When the Church is united, it can work more effectively to spread the Gospel, serve the poor, and bring about justice and peace.

- Acts 4:31-32: "And when they had prayed, the place where they were assembled together was shaken; and they were all filled with the Holy Spirit, and they spoke the word of God with boldness. Now the multitude of those who believed were of one heart and one soul; neither did anyone say that any of the things he possessed was his own, but they had all things in common."

The early Church's unity, fostered by the Holy Spirit, was a key factor in its ability to grow and to impact the world. The Spirit's empowerment for mission continues to be essential for the Church today, as believers work together to advance the Kingdom of God.

27.5.3 Unity in Diversity as a Model for the World

The unity in diversity that the Holy Spirit creates within the Church serves as a model for the world. In a world often marked by division and conflict, the Church's unity in diversity demonstrates the possibility of true reconciliation and peace.

- Galatians 3:28: "There is neither Jew nor Greek, there is neither slave nor free, there is neither male nor female; for you are all one in Christ Jesus."

The Church's unity, empowered by the Holy Spirit, transcends all human barriers, offering a vision of a reconciled humanity under the lordship of Jesus Christ. This unity is a powerful witness to the world of the reality of God's Kingdom and the hope that is found in Christ.

27.6 Conclusion

The Holy Spirit is the source and sustainer of Christian unity, bringing believers together in recognizing and worshiping Jesus as Lord. This unity is not uniformity but a unity in diversity, where different gifts, cultures, and traditions are brought together under the lordship of Christ. The Spirit's work in fostering unity is essential for the Church's mission, enabling it to witness effectively to the world and to embody the love, peace, and reconciliation that are at the heart of the Gospel.

As believers, we are called to maintain the unity of the Spirit in the bond of peace, recognizing that our unity is a gift from God and a testimony to the world of Jesus' lordship. By relying on the Holy Spirit, we can overcome divisions, celebrate diversity, and work together to fulfill the mission that Jesus has entrusted to His Church. In this way, the Church becomes a living witness to the power of the Holy Spirit and the reality of the Kingdom of God, drawing others to worship Jesus as Lord and to experience the transformative power of His grace.

CHAPTER 10

THE IMPORTANCE OF ACKNOWLEDGING JESUS AS DIVINE

Final Thoughts on the Significance of This Belief for Faith and Practice

28.1 Introduction

The divinity of Jesus Christ is not merely a theological concept but a fundamental truth that shapes the entirety of Christian faith and practice. Throughout this exploration, we have examined the scriptural, historical, and theological foundations for the belief in Jesus' divinity, as well as its implications for the life of the Church and individual believers. In this concluding chapter, we will reflect on the critical importance of acknowledging Jesus as divine, considering how this belief influences our understanding of God, our relationship with Him, and our daily Christian walk.

28.2 The Centrality of Jesus' Divinity to Christian Faith

The belief in the divinity of Jesus Christ is the cornerstone of Christian faith. It is the defining characteristic that sets Christianity apart from other religions and philosophical systems. Without the acknowledgment of Jesus as divine, the entire framework of Christian theology collapses, rendering the Gospel message powerless and the hope of salvation void.

28.2.1 The Revelation of God in Jesus Christ

Christianity teaches that Jesus is the full and final revelation of God. As the Word made flesh, Jesus perfectly reveals the nature, character, and will of God to humanity.

- John 1:14, 18: "And the Word became flesh and dwelt among us, and we beheld His glory, the glory as of the only begotten of the Father, full of grace and truth... No one has seen God at any time. The only begotten Son, who is in the bosom of the Father, He has declared Him."

By acknowledging Jesus as divine, we recognize that in Him, we encounter God Himself. Jesus is not merely a messenger or prophet; He is God incarnate. This belief assures us that we can know God personally and intimately, as Jesus has made Him known in a way that no other could.

28.2.2 The Basis of Salvation

The divinity of Jesus is essential to the Christian understanding of salvation. Only a divine Savior could bear the weight of the world's sin, fulfill the demands of divine justice, and offer eternal life to all who believe.

- Acts 4:12: "Nor is there salvation in any other, for there is no other name under heaven given among men by which we must be saved."

Salvation is possible only because Jesus, being fully God and fully man, could bridge the gap between a holy God and sinful humanity. His divine nature ensured that His sacrifice on the cross was sufficient to atone for sin, defeat death, and secure eternal redemption for all who trust in Him.

28.2.3 The Foundation of Christian Worship

The divinity of Jesus is also the foundation of Christian worship. Christians worship Jesus as Lord, recognizing Him as worthy of the same honor and adoration given to the Father.

- Revelation 5:12-13: "Saying with a loud voice: 'Worthy is the Lamb who was slain to receive power and riches and wisdom, and strength and honor and glory and blessing!' And every creature which is in heaven and on the earth and under the earth and such as are in the sea, and all that are in them, I heard saying: 'Blessing and honor and glory and power be to Him who sits on the throne, and to the Lamb, forever and ever!'"

The worship of Jesus as divine is not optional for Christians; it is a central aspect of the faith. To worship Jesus is to acknowledge His divine identity and to submit to His lordship. This worship is not merely a religious duty but a response of love and gratitude to the One who is our Creator, Redeemer, and King.

28.3 The Practical Implications of Jesus' Divinity

Acknowledging Jesus as divine has profound practical implications for the life of a believer. It shapes our understanding of discipleship, influences our ethical and moral decisions, and provides the foundation for our hope and trust in God.

28.3.1 Discipleship and Obedience to Jesus

If Jesus is divine, then He is not just a teacher to be admired but a Lord to be followed. Discipleship involves more than adhering to Jesus' teachings; it means surrendering our lives to His authority and obeying His commands.

- Matthew 28:18-20: "And Jesus came and spoke to them, saying, 'All authority has been given to Me in heaven and on earth. Go therefore and make disciples of all the nations, baptizing them in the name of the Father and of the Son and of the Holy Spirit, teaching them to observe all things that I have commanded you; and lo, I am with you always, even to the end of the age.'"

Discipleship is rooted in the acknowledgment of Jesus' authority as the divine Son of God. It calls for a commitment to follow Him, to learn from Him, and to live in a way that reflects His character and mission. This commitment is not just a matter of personal devotion but involves participating in the mission of the Church, sharing the Gospel, and making disciples of all nations.

28.3.2 Ethical and Moral Living

The divinity of Jesus also serves as the basis for Christian ethics and morality. As God incarnate, Jesus provides the perfect example of how we are to live, and His teachings are the ultimate standard for our conduct.

- John 14:6: "Jesus said to him, 'I am the way, the truth, and the life. No one comes to the Father except through Me.'"

By following Jesus, we are called to live according to the truth He embodies. This involves loving our neighbors, practicing justice, showing mercy, and living with integrity. Our moral decisions are guided by the example and teachings of Jesus, who, as the divine Logos, embodies the wisdom and righteousness of God.

28.3.3 Trust and Hope in Jesus

The acknowledgment of Jesus' divinity provides believers with a firm foundation for trust and hope. Knowing that Jesus is fully God assures us that He is able to fulfill His promises, that He is sovereign over all things, and that He will ultimately bring about the fulfillment of God's Kingdom.

- Colossians 1:15-17: "He is the image of the invisible God, the firstborn over all creation. For by Him all things were created that are in heaven and that are on earth, visible and invisible, whether thrones or dominions or principalities or powers. All things were created through Him and for Him. And He is before all things, and in Him all things consist."

Because Jesus is divine, we can trust in His power to sustain us, to guide us through life's challenges, and to bring us into eternal life. Our hope is not based on human wisdom or strength but on the unchanging nature of God, revealed in Jesus Christ.

28.4 The Impact on the Church's Mission and Witness

The Church's mission and witness are deeply rooted in the belief in Jesus' divinity. This belief shapes the way the Church understands its purpose, its message, and its role in the world.

28.4.1 Proclaiming the Gospel of Jesus Christ

The divinity of Jesus is central to the Gospel message. The Church is called to proclaim that Jesus is Lord, that He is the Son of God who came to save the world, and that through Him, all people can be reconciled to God.

- Romans 10:9: "That if you confess with your mouth the Lord Jesus and believe in your heart that God has raised Him from the dead, you will be saved."

The Church's mission is to bear witness to the truth of Jesus' divinity, to invite others to recognize Him as Lord, and to call people to faith in Him. This proclamation is not just a matter of doctrine but of life-changing truth that has the power to transform individuals and communities.

28.4.2 The Church as the Body of Christ

Acknowledging Jesus as divine also has implications for the Church's identity as the body of Christ. As the body of Christ, the Church is called to continue His work on earth, empowered by the Holy Spirit and guided by His teachings.

- Ephesians 1:22-23: "And He put all things under His feet, and gave Him to be head over all things to the church, which is His body, the fullness of Him who fills all in all."

The Church's unity, mission, and purpose are all grounded in the acknowledgment of Jesus as the divine head of the body. This recognition calls the Church to live in unity, to serve the world in love, and to reflect the character of Christ in all its actions.

28.4.3 The Witness of Christian Unity

Finally, the acknowledgment of Jesus' divinity is a unifying factor for the global Church. Despite differences in tradition, culture, and practice, Christians around the world are united by their shared belief in Jesus as Lord and God.

- Philippians 2:10-11: "That at the name of Jesus every knee should bow, of those in heaven, and of those on earth, and of those under the earth, and that every tongue should confess that Jesus Christ is Lord, to the glory of God the Father."

Christian unity, grounded in the shared recognition of Jesus' divinity, is a powerful witness to the world. It demonstrates the truth of the Gospel and the reality of God's Kingdom, offering a vision of reconciliation and peace that transcends all human divisions.

28.5 Conclusion

The belief in Jesus' divinity is not merely a doctrinal point but the very heart of the Christian faith. It shapes our understanding of who God is, how we relate to Him, and how we live our lives. Acknowledging Jesus as divine is essential for our salvation, our worship, our discipleship, and our witness to the world.

As we conclude this exploration of Jesus' divinity, we are reminded of the profound impact that this belief has on every aspect of the Christian life. It calls us to a deeper relationship with God, a more committed discipleship, a life of ethical integrity, and a bold witness to the truth of the Gospel.

May we continue to honor Jesus as Lord and God, living in the light of His divinity, and proclaiming His name to all the world. In doing so, we participate in the great mission of the Church, bringing glory to God and extending His Kingdom on earth.

A Call to Faith

Encouraging Readers to Deepen Their Faith in Jesus Christ as the Son of God and Savior

29.1 Introduction

Faith in Jesus Christ as the Son of God and Savior is the foundation of the Christian life. It is through faith that we enter into a relationship with God, experience His grace, and receive the gift of eternal life. This chapter is a call to deepen that faith, to trust more fully in Jesus, and to embrace Him as the Lord of our lives. Whether you are new to the Christian faith or have walked with Jesus for many years, there is always room to grow, to know Him more intimately, and to live more fully in the light of His love and truth.

29.2 The Essential Nature of Faith in Jesus Christ

Faith in Jesus is not just an intellectual agreement with certain doctrines; it is a living, dynamic relationship with the living God. It is the response of the heart and mind to the revelation of Jesus as the Son of God and the Savior of the world.

29.2.1 Faith as Trust in Jesus

At its core, faith is trust—trusting that Jesus is who He says He is, that He has done what He promised to do, and that He will fulfill all His promises to us. It is trusting that He is the way, the truth, and the life, and that no one comes to the Father except through Him (John 14:6).

- Proverbs 3:5-6: "Trust in the Lord with all your heart, and lean not on your own understanding; in all your ways acknowledge Him, and He shall direct your paths."

Faith involves surrendering our own understanding and control, and placing our trust entirely in Jesus. It means believing that He knows what is best for us, that He is faithful to His word, and that He will lead us on the path of life.

29.2.2 Faith as Relationship with Jesus

Faith is also about relationship—a deep, personal connection with Jesus Christ. It is through faith that we enter into this relationship, where we come to know Jesus not just as a distant figure from history, but as our living Lord and Savior.

- John 17:3: "And this is eternal life, that they may know You, the only true God, and Jesus Christ whom You have sent."

To know Jesus is to have eternal life. This knowledge is not merely intellectual but experiential—it is the kind of knowing that comes from walking with Him daily, listening to His voice, and following His lead. It is a relationship that transforms every aspect of our lives.

29.2.3 Faith as the Foundation of Salvation

Faith in Jesus is the means by which we receive salvation. It is by grace through faith that we are saved, and this faith is the assurance of things hoped for, the conviction of things not seen (Hebrews 11:1).

- Ephesians 2:8-9: "For by grace you have been saved through faith, and that not of yourselves; it is the gift of God, not of works, lest anyone should boast."

Salvation is not something we can earn through our own efforts; it is a gift that we receive by faith. This faith acknowledges that Jesus' death and resurrection are sufficient to atone for our sins, reconcile us to God, and give us the hope of eternal life.

29.3 The Call to Deepen Your Faith

As believers, we are called to grow in our faith, to deepen our trust in Jesus, and to pursue a closer relationship with Him. This growth in faith is not a one-time event but a lifelong journey.

29.3.1 Growing in the Knowledge of Jesus

One of the ways we deepen our faith is by growing in our knowledge of Jesus. This involves studying the Scriptures, spending time in prayer, and reflecting on the truths of the Gospel.

- Colossians 1:9-10: "For this reason we also, since the day we heard it, do not cease to pray for you, and to ask that you may be filled with the knowledge of His will in all wisdom and spiritual understanding; that you may walk worthy of the Lord, fully pleasing Him, being fruitful in every good work and increasing in the knowledge of God."

As we increase in our knowledge of Jesus, we are better equipped to trust Him in all areas of our lives. This knowledge is not just academic but transformative, shaping our character and guiding our decisions.

29.3.2 Persevering in Faith Through Trials

Faith is often tested in the crucible of trials and challenges. It is in these moments that our trust in Jesus is deepened, as we learn to rely on Him in the midst of difficulties.

- James 1:2-4: "My brethren, count it all joy when you fall into various trials, knowing that the testing of your faith produces patience. But let patience have its perfect work, that you may be perfect and complete, lacking nothing."

Trials are opportunities to grow in faith, as they force us to depend more fully on God and to trust in His goodness, even when circumstances are difficult. Through perseverance, our faith is strengthened, and we are drawn closer to Jesus.

29.3.3 Living Out Your Faith in Daily Life

Faith in Jesus is not just a private matter; it is meant to be lived out in every aspect of our lives. This involves following Jesus' example, loving others as He has loved us, and being His witnesses in the world.

- James 2:17: "Thus also faith by itself, if it does not have works, is dead."

True faith results in action—it leads us to live out the teachings of Jesus in practical ways, serving others, seeking justice, and proclaiming the Gospel. As we live out our faith, we become more like Christ and bring His love and truth to those around us.

29.4 Encouragement to Strengthen Your Faith

As we conclude this journey of exploring the divinity of Jesus and the implications of this truth for our lives, I encourage you to take steps to strengthen your faith, to trust Jesus more fully, and to grow in your relationship with Him.

29.4.1 Trust in Jesus' Unfailing Love

No matter where you are in your faith journey, you can trust in Jesus' unfailing love. He is faithful, and He will never leave you or forsake you.

- Romans 8:38-39: "For I am persuaded that neither death nor life, nor angels nor principalities nor powers, nor things present nor things to come, nor height nor depth, nor any other created thing, shall be able to separate us from the love of God which is in Christ Jesus our Lord."

Jesus' love is constant and unchanging. It is a love that pursues us, forgives us, and redeems us. As you place your trust in His love, you will find security, peace, and joy that transcends all circumstances.

29.4.2 Seek to Know Jesus More Intimately

Make it your goal to know Jesus more intimately. Spend time with Him in prayer, immerse yourself in His Word, and seek His presence daily.

- Philippians 3:10: "That I may know Him and the power of His resurrection, and the fellowship of His sufferings, being conformed to His death."

The more you know Jesus, the deeper your faith will become. This knowledge will transform your life, filling you with the power of His resurrection and the assurance of His presence.

29.4.3 Share Your Faith with Others

Faith in Jesus is a gift that is meant to be shared. As you grow in your faith, look for opportunities to share the hope of the Gospel with others, to be a witness to the love and truth of Jesus Christ.

- 1 Peter 3:15: "But sanctify the Lord God in your hearts, and always be ready to give a defense to everyone who asks you a reason for the hope that is in you, with meekness and fear."

Sharing your faith not only strengthens your own belief but also brings others into the joy of knowing Jesus. It is through the testimony of our lives and words that the light of Christ shines in the world.

29.5 Conclusion

Faith in Jesus Christ as the Son of God and Savior is the bedrock of the Christian life. It is the key that unlocks the door to a relationship with God, the source of our salvation, and the foundation for our daily walk with the Lord. As you continue on your journey of faith, I encourage you to deepen your trust in Jesus, to seek Him with all your heart, and to live out your faith in every area of your life.

Jesus is calling you to a deeper faith, a faith that is rooted in His divinity, sustained by His love, and expressed in a life of obedience and service. Respond to that call with an open heart, trusting that He will lead you, sustain you, and fill you with His peace and joy. As you do, you will experience the fullness of life that Jesus offers—a life that is abundant, eternal, and grounded in the unshakable truth that He is Lord and Savior.